Affirm
press

Tim and Rod became two of the most-loved faces on Aussie television when they won Network 10's *The Amazing Race* in 2019. As the first gay married couple on Australian TV, they loved inspiring the LGBTIQA+ community and normalising the appearance of queer people in prime time. Aside from television, the pair have launched *The Real Househusbands* podcast series, celebrating their guilty pleasure of reality TV, as well as maintaining a social-media presence that includes more than 87k followers on Instagram. Through their stories and oversharing, Tim and Rod are devoted to encouraging all young people to embrace who they are, no matter how different from the mainstream, usually by having a good laugh at their own expense. Tim and Rod live in Newcastle, New South Wales, and *The Greatest Feeling in the World* is their first book.

The GREATEST FEELING in the WORLD

Affirmpress
books that leave an impression

Published by Affirm Press in 2021
28 Thistlethwaite Street, South Melbourne,
Boon Wurrung Country, VIC 3205
affirmpress.com.au
10 9 8 7 6 5 4 3 2 1

Every effort has been made to trace copyright holders and to obtain their
permission for the use of copyright material. The publisher apologises for any
errors or omissions and would be grateful if notified of any corrections that
should be incorporated in the final printed edition or future editions and
reprints of this book.

 A catalogue record for this
book is available from the
National Library of Australia

Title: The Greatest Feeling in the World / Tim and Rod Sattler-Jones, authors.
ISBN: 9781922626226 (paperback)
Cover design by Luke Causby/Blue Cork
Cover photograph by Andrew Simington
Typeset in Adobe Garamond Pro by J&M Typesetting
Proudly printed in Australia by Griffin Press

 The paper this book is printed on is certified against the
Forest Stewardship Council® Standards. Griffin Press holds
chain of custody certification SGSHK-COC-005088. FSC®
promotes environmentally responsible, socially beneficial
and economically viable management of the world's forests.

We would like to dedicate this book to our younger selves. Thank you for not giving up and for finding the courage and strength to be your true, authentic selves. One day you will meet your Prince Charming, who will love you for all your quirks and for not being afraid to be 'Different'.

Contents

Prologue

TIM

THIS IS IT. We are about to get married and live happily ever after!

Well, kind of. To quote Shakespeare (former theatre geek that I am), 'The course of true love never did run smooth,' and that is certainly true for us. But the issues in our relationship rarely come from within.

When the Sattlers are on board, they are 100 per cent on board. Everyone wants in on the wedding action. Mum's going to walk me down the aisle, my brothers Ben and Trent are my best men, Aunty Jenza is our celebrant, my cousin Amy and her boyfriend are doing the music, my nephew Winston is our ringbearer and, most importantly, Uncle Damo is on standby for any emergency bottle-o runs.

I am so full of pride; not only am I ready to fly the rainbow flag as one of the first gay people to be legally married in Australia, but I am also beyond proud to come from a family who would do anything in their power to support me. Yet I'm trying to downplay their roles in the wedding because the more they contribute, the more it seems to underline the absence of Rod's family.

As much as Rod is being his strong, steadfast self, it's obvious to me that he is hurting. A lot. His family's distinct lack of interest and excitement is clear. Their strong judgement is ever-present. They wholeheartedly believe that we're sinful and that two men should *not* get married.

I don't ever want to make this about me, but I can't help feeling humiliated and confused by the fact that Rod's family are so against us getting married. The guilt weighs heavily on my heart. I also struggle to understand why they feel this way. Do they really believe their God doesn't approve of same-sex marriage?

With Rod's family, I feel like an outcast. I've known that because I'm a gay man they'll always keep me at a distance, but I'd thought they would be able to separate me as a person from my gender and sexuality. Apparently not. I am clearly not what they want for their son and they shun me in the hope I'll be replaced by a woman – any woman. For someone who has always felt rejected and alienated, I find this fucking hard.

This does not fit with my fairytale ending at all.

ROD

We're about to get married and my Prince Charming is waiting on the other side of the rope bridge. But in my way is a dragon in the shape of my family's rejection.

'Mum and I are having a hard time coming to terms with you marrying a bloke,' my dad tells me.

What?

'Mate, it's nothing to do with Tim, it could be any bloke. We just don't think it's right.'

Meeting Tim had helped mend my heart, broken by family rejection. Now it's shattering all over again.

My parents refused to show at our engagement party. They also ensured my brother and grandparents didn't attend either. What's more, they told me flat out that a wedding was out of the question. There is no way in the world Mum's Christian beliefs will ever let her attend a same-sex wedding. My parents think that being gay is a choice and that gay marriage is wrong.

Does my happiness just not matter? This and so many other questions bounce around my head on countless sleepless nights as the wedding approaches. I want all of my family there and for them to, just this once, celebrate me for being me. To be happy for me.

I try to tell myself and everyone around me that my anxiety and doubts are normal, it's just '21st-century gay wedding' cold feet from all the wedding planning and stress. Not to say I'm not having some very real wedding stress – I mean, what even *is* a 'gay wedding'? Same-sex marriage has only recently been legalised in Australia and neither of us has ever been to a gay wedding. We have no idea what we're doing!

We want to show the world that our love is just as important as any other couple's and that it's our right to call it marriage. But we also want to show off! We feel intense pressure to have this extravagant event, a stereotype to live up to, a hectic dance break at the reception that will go viral online and the most boujee set-up you have ever seen. We need to set a precedent, a high bar for all gay weddings to follow.

It's also an amazing time and we're so happy. But every time I get excited, I think, *If my family aren't going to be there, what's the point? How can I give myself completely to someone if it means leaving behind such a big part of who I am?*

1

TIM: 'That's so gay'

My school life is so shit. It does have some high points – mostly just the school holidays – but it's mainly riddled with bullying, insults and insecurity. Being a gay kid is tough and being a gay kid in Newcastle is tougher still. It's a huge coal town with a rough exterior. Everyone seems to know one another so there's just no place to hide. Not only am I struggling with the fact that I'm 'different', but that difference is also pointed out to me daily in Year 6.

Why do you act like a girl? You're such a fairy. That's so gay! You scream like a girl. You've got to be a faggot, right? We don't want a sissy on our team.

The more that the kids in class, at recess and lunch, and on the oval drill home that I'm different or weird, the more I'm starting to believe they're right. Worse, I'm starting to think that being different is wrong.

I'd do anything to make the bullying stop and I just want to be like everyone else. Instead, I feel like a freak who doesn't deserve to be alive and, on some very dark days, I want to leave this world completely, to simply escape the pain. It's soul-destroying to be made fun of and ridiculed for just being myself. Nothing I do is right. I hate sport but love dancing, I hate video games but love acting, I hate playing cops and robbers and instead I'm obsessed with art and craft. All the other boys want to be famous soccer players and I just want to be one of the Spice Girls: Scary, of course! I want to wear her outfits, walk in her shoes, have big hair and perform confidently in front of thousands of people like she does.

If my interests aren't enough of a giveaway that I'm different, then the hand-me-down clothes that I've covered in glitter and stick-on diamantés would certainly confirm it. I'm an outcast and there seems to be nothing I can do about it.

Every day at school I find myself walking around eating lunch to save myself the humiliation of sitting alone. I can't shake the overwhelming fear and embarrassment of clearly being different. As I do continuous laps of the schoolyard while eating my sandwich, I look around at all the other kids. Everyone has their private cliques and bestie groups. It's my worst nightmare to run around with the boys in the scorching-hot sun and as much as I'd like to sit in the shade with the girls talking about Britney Spears, who I've recently become obsessed with, there's no way in hell they'll accept me. I secretly bought her first album, *Baby One More Time*, and am playing it non-stop on my Discman. I'd love to talk to the girls about Britney's dance-break routines and amazing costumes, or about the *Titanic* movie. (I desperately want to be Rose and have a Jack to sweep me off my feet!) Anyway, the girls'd just say, 'Why would a boy want to sit with us?'

As I pace the blazing concrete, I can't wait for the lunchtime bell to ring and put me out of my misery. Sometimes after doing a lap of the school for what feels like the hundredth time, my feet are sore and I need to sit down. I'm not going to sit down by myself in plain sight, that's for sure, so the only place to go is the boys' toilets.

Walking into the toilet cubicle, I'm confronted with the most disgusting smell and hundreds of flies. This is the last place I want to be. Most of the other kids live for recess and lunchtime fun with their friends, but here I am in the toilets, afraid and embarrassed, waiting for the bell to ring and rescue me from this stinking, filthy, gross coffin I've locked myself in.

Pacing the school on my own, I've had plenty of time to observe how the social world works. I know that if I want to be like all the other boys, I need to pretend that I enjoy playing sports. When the lunchtime bell rings, all the boys rush to team up and play never-ending rounds of soccer, footy, cricket, basketball, handball. Meanwhile I would rather play Barbies with the girls and see what bits Ken has under his clothes. But if I want to stop the insults, protect myself a bit and finally make some friends, I need to make the other boys believe I'm a sports super fan.

I muster up as much courage as I possibly can and reluctantly walk over to the soccer pitch – court? *Oh my God I don't even know what it's called* – where all the boys are playing soccer. I stand there on the sideline, watching them play together so effortlessly, my stomach a bundle of nerves. The voices in my head tell me I'm never going to fit in and this is a stupid idea, but the desire to be like everyone else is way too strong to ignore.

I nervously walk up to one of the coolest boys at my school, Alex, and mutter, 'Can I please join in?' His jaw drops open. He looks around at all the other boys to see if anyone's going to confirm that I'm serious. I knew this was a bad idea. I start to backpedal to avoid total embarrassment: 'I can just be a goalie, so I don't get in the way of everyone.'

Alex hesitates, then probably to avoid awkwardness he just goes, 'Yeah I guess so.'

This is it: I finally have an opportunity to fit in. I know my soccer skills aren't going to change the world, but how hard can it be to stop a ball from entering a net? As I walk towards the goal, I see the other team all trying to hide their smiles. They clearly believe they're now going to win, but I'm determined to prove Alex and his mates wrong. This is my time to shine and show the entire schoolyard that even though I like drama, dance and playing imaginary shopping games with the girls, I can also totally smash it on the soccer field.

Alex aggressively throws the ball down and the game is back in action. My heart starts racing a million miles an hour. What if the ball hits me in the face? What if I kick it and break my ankle? What if it smashes me in the chest and my heart stops and I die? I stand there like a deer in headlights, praying the ball doesn't come anywhere near me. In fact I wish it would spontaneously pop and the game would be called off forever.

Instead the ball starts hurtling directly towards me at the speed of light.

Oh my God oh my God! I scream in my head. I know that if I stuff this up, I'll be humiliated in front of everyone and once again the butt of everyone's jokes. So I close my eyes, let out a scream and jerk my leg in what I think is the direction of the ball.

Nothing happens. I slowly open my eyes, look around and realise the ball has flown straight past me and into the goal. I look back and all the other boys are laughing and pointing at what they've just witnessed. Not only have I just let out the most high-pitched scream in the history of the schoolyard but I've also lost the deciding point. I stand there feeling totally embarrassed when suddenly the bell rings.

Yay, I think, *saved by the bell.*

The other boys run back to class, still chuckling, while I hang my head in shame and hurry back to the boys' toilets. I feel like I'm going to burst into tears and don't want anyone to see me looking even more pathetic than I already do.

The one place I can be myself is dance class. Dance and performing arts are the only things that fill me with joy and allow me to truly be myself. I feel like I can survive the school day, all the insults, all the exclusion, because I know that for those few hours a week

5

I can escape and just be happy. Without that, I don't think I'd make it through.

I'm obsessed with making up dance routines and I choreograph entire Super Bowl performances in the privacy of my bedroom. I need my hit of dance every day and if I don't get it, I feel like I'll explode. I continually beg my parents to let me be part of the yearly school dance concerts and get so excited when I receive outrageous outfits. I'm fixated on all the bright colours, glitter and sparkles.

My parents never tell me I'm not allowed to dance. My mum wholeheartedly encourages and supports me to pursue my creative interests and even enrols me in dance lessons, a craft group and a weekly drama class. Mum is the most genuine and kind-hearted person you could ever meet. She's a kindergarten teacher and so passionate about her job; her other main mission in life is to make the people around her happy. Wherever she goes and whatever she does, she's always spreading positive vibes.

My favourite weekend outing is going to Spotlight with Mum to pick out the most over-the-top material I can get my hands on. On the drive I'm not sure if I'm more excited going shopping with Mum or driving past the enormous penis-shaped observation tower that Newcastle's famous for. As we arrive in the city we can see the smoke billowing out of the coal-plant chimneys and we hear the horns of huge coal ships entering Newcastle Harbour.

In Spotlight, I run around like a headless chicken. We spend hours showing each other fabrics, the brighter and more outrageous the better. Mum sparks up conversations with other customers like she always does. She loves meeting new people and learning about their lives. Dad often says, 'Your mother can talk underwater with a mouth full of marbles,' which is so true.

Even though I always feel I have Mum's complete support, it's a different story with my dad and two older brothers. They're the definition of 'Aussie men'. My brothers Ben and Trent are the cool, popular kids in school, stars of the local rugby league team and surf competitions. While I'm practising dance routines, they're playing rugby; when I'm at craft group, they're surfing; and I'm in drama class when they're at soccer practice. We have nothing in common and I struggle to relate to them in any way. Even though they accept me, I'm always enormously ashamed that I'm not like them.

Dad's a builder but he suffered a bad work injury when I was young. He fell off a ladder and broke his leg badly; his leg has never fully recovered and his life has been seriously affected by it. No son wants to let his father down and I always feel like my dad would be a lot prouder of me if I was more like my brothers.

While he's always there for me, I still worry that I'm failing him as a son. Everywhere I look, I see families just like mine, living in houses just like mine, with blokey dads just like mine and sons ... well, nothing like me! Dad comes to my dance shows to cheer me on and to make me feel loved and supported, but deep down I wonder how he really feels.

Like everyone else in Year 6, I'm obsessed with *Baywatch*. Why wouldn't I be? It's a TV show about ultra-hot people running up and down a California beach in red swimwear.

Dad has only recently paid for a yearly Foxtel subscription and one lazy afternoon I'm sitting alone flicking through the hundreds of channels, desperate to find something to fill my boredom. My brothers are of course outside, skating up and down the street with their best friends.

As I mindlessly flick through the channels something catches my eye and I stop, fixated. It's an episode of *Baywatch*, and I've changed the channel at the exact moment Cody Madison is working out at the beach. Cody is one of the red speedo–wearing hotties on the show: incredibly beautiful and lean with the cutest smile I have ever seen. His exquisite golden locks never look out of place, even while working out. He is my idea of perfection. And I cannot believe what I'm seeing.

Mesmerised by his washboard abs and perfectly tanned skin, I slink off the couch onto the floor, directly in front of the TV. I'm instantly transported to my ultimate Malibu fantasy; I can almost feel the salty air on my skin and smell the coconut oil dripping off Cody's body.

I've never felt this way about anyone before. I want to be like him. Wait, maybe more? I'm confused. Lost in my imagination, I begin to fantasise about him rescuing me from the ocean. He runs along the beach in signature *Baywatch* slow motion, his athletic body cuts through the water towards me, his muscular arms reaching for me, then he throws me on my back, grabs me tight and powerfully swims me to safety.

I become incredibly turned on.

My head filled with thoughts of Cody, his smile and his muscles, I run to my room and start to touch myself. It feels great. I just keep going with the flow. With two older brothers in the house, I know what masturbation is, but knowing about it and doing it are two totally different things. The magazines they have are full of women, and looking at those glossy images never makes me feel this way.

Suddenly it dawns on me that I'm touching myself while thinking of a man! Am I really masturbating while thinking about Cody from *Baywatch*? Should I quickly change to thinking of Pamela's boobs instead? No way, I want Cody! It feels too good to stop, so I don't. *This is what everyone was talking about*, I think. My imagination is running wild, my body is following its lead and it feels amazing, I keep going and it's incredible. Then – boom.

HOLY SHIT!

As I sink back into the pillow, a wave of relaxation washes over me. That was unbelievable. I promise myself to take note of every day and time Cody will grace my TV screen and that I won't miss a single second. From that moment on, *Baywatch* – okay, Cody – becomes my newfound obsession. And in temporarily escaping into that sun-kissed fantasy, I felt released from any awkwardness, shame or embarrassment.

For a moment.

Fear, guilt and sadness come crashing back in, taking me over in the same way the intense pleasure did just a few minutes ago. *Oh. My. God.* What have I just done? I am disgusted with myself. No one can ever know what just happened. This will be my secret forever.

The next day at school, I try to put the whole thing behind me. In the corridor I comment to a boy in my class how amazing Pamela Anderson's boobs are. He starts nodding but then looks up, realises it's me who said this and looks confused. I'm obviously the last person he expected to hear this from. In an awkward moment I wish I could forget, he mutters, 'Yeah she's got nice tits,' and quickly walks away.

Still, this attempt does make me feel a little better, and in some weird and twisted way, gives me a bit of hope that no one will ever find out my deep dark *Baywatch* secret. I just need to learn to perfect more believable Pamela Anderson compliments.

2

ROD: 'Not Adam and Steve'

My pop is the most important man in my life. My dad is a shift worker so I don't see much of him. He works nights in the mines that feed the coal trains running through the city to the harbour. I spend more time with Pop. It's Pop who teaches me how to peel prawns; in my family you learn how to do it quickly or you miss out.

Pop looks out for everyone – he's the warmest, most caring person and totally devoted to his kids and grandkids. He kisses and cuddles us all the time and always makes a point of kissing his sons and grandsons. We hear Nan before we see her because she has such a big laugh, and she always seems happy. Nan and Pop are so involved in all our lives.

Until one day, Pop isn't.

Nan and Pop were on holidays with friends up at South West Rocks on the Mid North Coast. Pop went out fishing with his mates on the boat and had a heart attack. He was sixty. Nan's fifty-four.

Pop's death hits my mum hard. Mum's gorgeous, with her

curly black hair and the most beautiful olive skin she got from Pop, who was Maltese. She goes from being this fun-loving, active, happy preschool teacher to someone unrecognisable. It's as if her mind can't take the fact that she has lost someone so dear to her. She starts staying in bed all day.

I don't really understand what's going on with her, but I know I love her and I want to help. Each morning, I wake up and make Mum her Weet-Bix and a cup of tea. I place it all on a big serving platter decorated with flowers and deliver it to her upstairs. I carry it ever so carefully into her room and place it on the bedside table, then I help her sit up and place these huge blue decorative pillows behind her back. I always remove the tea bag because she hates her tea too strong. Then I jump into bed next to her, turn on the TV and ... watch Pokémon, my favourite show ever. That, Mum just has to endure.

Even though she is sad, Mum always forces a smile when I walk in each morning.

She's on medication and she doesn't want to feel this way anymore.

Nan thinks Mum should go to church. It takes some convincing, but eventually Mum agrees to give it a go.

When Mum comes home she tells me the pastor had talked about heaven and never being alone. He described being a Christian and having a relationship with God like having someone looking out for you all the time. The thing that really made an impression, though, was what the pastor said about being reunited with your loved ones in heaven after you die, which was like music to Mum's ears.

The pastor's message gives Mum hope and something to live for again. She becomes a born-again Christian and commits her life to God, and from that day on we attend the local Baptist Church every Sunday.

All I know is that Mum's decision to turn to God saved her life. She quickly goes from being sad all the time, bedridden and on heavy medication to being a strong, beautiful woman who no longer needs medication at all. I have my mum back again, and it makes me believe in miracles.

Church is okay. It's an incredibly old brick building with stained-glass windows that reach from the floor to the ceiling. Inside are long, hard wooden pews, a stage with a lectern the pastor preaches from and an enormous gold cross on the wall at the front of the church with the words HE IS RISEN above it. I usually stay in church for a bit of music and worship then head out to the Kids Club and play with the other kids.

By the time I'm eleven Kids Club doesn't amuse me anymore, so I stay in church for the entire hour-long service and listen to the pastor preach each week.

Seems like church is a bunch of rules that we have to live by, or else!

If it's not 'Do not lie or steal', it's 'Do not swear or use God's name in vain'. The list – or 'commandments' as the Bible calls it – goes on and on. 'Don't murder.' 'Honour your mother and father.' 'No sex before marriage.'

I feel like church is teaching me how to be a 'good', respectable person. It's not that hard not to lie, steal and murder; I respect my parents and am mostly a well-behaved kid. I am not even thinking about sex; in fact, the word 'sex' makes me giggle. I say 'hump' or 'doing it' instead and think 'penis' and 'vagina' are swear words.

The Senior Pastor is a cranky old dude with thinning, partly grey, partly white, partly brown hair combed over to the side. Every week he makes his entrance from the foyer at the back of the church and struts down the aisle between the rows of wooden pews. He has his Bible in one hand and never makes eye contact with anyone as he makes his way to the stage. He walks up the three steps at the front to get to the lectern, puts his things down, fixes his glasses with his thumb, walks on the spot a few times, hitches his pants then says, 'Let's pray.' It's the same every single week.

Most of the time the pastor stays behind the lectern while he preaches, but when it's time to make a point, he paces from one side of the stage to the other using a lot of hand gestures, stops for one his infamous 'walks on the spot', then delivers his punchline. This routine must work because I always feel like the entire message is aimed at me when he moves away from his lectern and I swear he makes hectic eye contact with me when making his point. I may not know what he is talking about, but I am paying attention to that punchline!

I have no idea why the pastor is looking at me when he preaches or why, week after week, I seem to be hearing the same message.

'Man must marry a Woman.'

Yes, that makes sense. Everyone I know has a mum and dad. I have aunties and uncles. Every movie, book and fairytale has a prince and a princess who fall in love. I want to fall in love and get married, but I don't understand why the pastor's statement makes my armpits sweat and my heart rate increase, or why he is looking into my soul when he says it. There's this old gold clock on the wall and every time the pastor looks directly at me, I quickly look up at the clock to break eye contact.

The other frequently preached statement is 'Sinners will go to Hell'. In fact, in church they speak more of hell than they ever do of heaven. It's this evil place where the devil lives, filled with fire and brimstone. The pastor describes hell as a place where you will be alone, hearing all your loved ones screaming in pain for eternity and you will be helpless with no way to reach them. This is petrifying for me. The pastor teaches that 'if you are not in a committed relationship with God then you will burn for eternity', 'we must ask for forgiveness' and 'God is the only one who can save you'. I even learn that 'good' people will still go to hell if they don't have a personal relationship with Christ or become a born-again Christian.

Scarily, I have started realising that I am different, which makes me extra worried about hell. I don't really understand the term 'gay'; all I know is that I have an admiration for men. But I also have a sinking feeling that this puts me in the sinner camp …

At the end of Year 5, my sister Emma and I are offered a scholarship to a private Christian school. A woman from church passed away and her will provided for two children to be put through the Christian school. It's an expensive school with a good reputation and way too good an opportunity to turn down. It's not so bad for Emma because she was about to go into Year 7 and needed to change schools anyway, but I've just been made school captain so it's a bigger deal for me to leave. But it's both of us or neither, so I have to go.

Mum and Dad tell me that we'll start there in the new year, which is a bummer as I have to turn down the school captaincy. I'm upset about that because I totally smashed it in my speech to get that role. It also means I have to dump my girlfriend, Karen, because 'a long-distance relationship just isn't going to work for me'. My school will be fifteen minutes away.

I don't think the new school will be that different, but boy am I wrong. This school is strict; uniform has to be perfect, and we even have to wear matching school bags which are soooo ugly. We have a subject called Prayer and Praise, and they don't even teach religion – it's called biblical studies, which is compulsory by the way. We pray during roll call and at the beginning of many classes. I'm not in my small public school anymore.

The school is an old mine colliery converted into a school and owned by the Baptist Church we're attending; the toilets are the original washrooms. But it's now a very expensive place to attend. I'm embarrassed about telling people I got a scholarship so I just keep it secret.

It takes a bit to settle in. It seems strange to me that the majority of the kids attending this school are from Christian homes and from families that attend and are regular members of a church, until I find out that this is a requirement. Suddenly, without me even realising it, my life has become Christian. School, church, home, friends – everything has an underlying Christian teaching.

I don't mind. I enjoy my new school and have become friends with the cool group and seem to fit in. I have scored myself a new girlfriend, one of the prettiest girls in school. We pass love letters in class then hold hands in the playground until the teachers tells us to stop. After school I give her a peck on the cheek and think I am so cool.

Except … I don't actually want to kiss her, I just feel like it's what I'm meant to do. I'm actually going home from school daydreaming about the popular boys a couple of years older than me, not thinking about the soft cheek of my girlfriend. This is my secret, and it doesn't mean anything.

I can't help what I think about, I just won't act on it, I keep saying to myself over and over.

Meanwhile, from every angle, the messages I am getting are 'Find a nice girl, get married young, have kids and get a golden retriever' or 'Dedicate your life to the Lord, spread the message of Jesus and do God's Work'.

The phrases 'you're Gay' or 'that's Gay' are thrown around all the time. The people saying it don't mean it literally; it's more a figure of speech, but for the first time in my life I'm starting to put the pieces of the puzzle together. I start wondering, 'What is a Gay person?' 'How do you become Gay?' 'Can you choose not to be?'

There is an ongoing joke at school that for some reason really rattles me.

'GOD MADE ADAM AND EVE, NOT ADAM AND STEVE!'

I have no idea why this joke gets to me so badly. All I know is that I do not want to be feeling this way and I definitely do not want to be Gay. I feel like a crazy person. I want to get married and have kids, I want to have a girlfriend in school, I want to be making out with girls behind the demountable classrooms like the other kids, but everything in my being is screaming *No!* There is a tug of war between my brain and every other part of me.

Every so often at church, people choose to be baptised. As I sit in church and watch these people get dunked in water, I want to know more. I ask for a meeting with the youth pastor to find out more about it. Sitting in a small room at the back of the church, the youth pastor explains that for a born-again Christian, baptism symbolises being washed clean. I am holding onto every word he says. He continues to explain that as you enter the baptismal waters, you leave your old self and sins behind and as you go under the water you are washed clean and rise as a new person.

This is it! 'I want to be baptised,' I announce to the youth pastor. Surely the holy baptismal waters can wash my mind clean, and I won't think this way anymore. My confusing thoughts can be washed down the drain with all my sins.

I prepare my testimony, to read out loud to the congregation before my baptism. On the day, I nervously state that God has saved my mum and that I want to dedicate my life to Him. There is no way I am going to say why I'm really doing this. Even as I speak, my anxious mind is puzzling, *Will my baptism work if I lie about the reasons I want it?* As I complete my testimony the congregation is clapping for me. The youth pastor prays over me, then, with his hand on my head, pushes me under the water and I rise a new, clean person.

I wish. As I stand there dripping, my heart sinks and I know, it didn't work; I'm still me.

Back to the drawing board.

Many of the kids at school go to Pentecostal churches. They talk about the cool music they play, speaking in tongues, miracles and healings. They tell me about youth group on Friday nights and I decide I have to check it out. If these guys can pray for me and get rid of my confusing thoughts, then count me in.

During youth group they encourage people to come down and be prayed for by the youth pastor. He asks what I would like him to pray for and I mumble something generic about sinful thoughts. The pastor lays his hands on my head, speaks in tongues and tells me to give all my worries over to the Lord. All I can hear in my head while he speaks is:

GOD MADE ADAM AND EVE, NOT ADAM AND STEVE

GOD MADE ADAM AND EVE, NOT ADAM AND STEVE

GOD MADE ADAM AND EVE, NOT ADAM AND STEVE

He stops. I open my eyes. It didn't work.

I'm going to a good school, I have amazing parents, I'm going to church and youth group and have the best friends in the world. Everything is perfect except for the feelings and voices in my head that just will not go away.

I repeat to myself every single day, *You like girls.* If I do not like girls then why do I have girlfriends? I try to convince myself this is true, but the voices in my head tell me otherwise.

Every day I catch my eyes wandering to this guy's muscles or that teacher's bulge, and the voices start all over again. *You like that, don't you, You can look, That's so hot.*

I find myself daydreaming about boys in class then realise I need to conceal the boner raging through my shorts under the table.

Each week in church I sit there and am told that 'God can heal anyone or anything' and 'God forgives all'. But why aren't I being healed?

I have now been baptised and prayed for a hundred times.

I cannot keep going down for prayers that don't work and if I keep responding, people are going to get suss.

The Church would have me believe that the voices in my head are the Devil trying to trick me into being attracted to men. But the feeling seems to come from much deeper within my soul.

I'm conforming to what my new world tells me is 'right' but why is it making me feel so wrong? Why is it making me feel like something's wrong with me? Why is it making me feel like I'm sinning? I'm so scared that if I keep thinking like this, I am going to hell.

3

TIM: Thank God my balls have dropped

I have never wanted anything more in my life; I want it so bad it hurts. I have waited and waited for years and now it's finally happening I'm over the moon: my balls are starting to drop.

I'm overwhelmed with happiness as my voice begins to change. I've always had a high-pitched, feminine voice and my laugh sounds like I've inhaled a full tank of helium. My mannerisms are also flamboyant and my physical characteristics very feminine (explaining why I'm mistaken for a girl at school most days). Basically, I have G-A-Y tattooed across my forehead in huge letters for all to see. I'm so relieved that my body is changing, and I've started developing stereotypical male characteristics. Being gay is going to be a whole lot easier to hide thanks to my new best mate, puberty.

I start sprouting crazy amounts of pubic hair and my testicles grow as well as drop. I have an insanely rapid growth spurt and become one of the tallest people in my school year. My entire body shape is transforming: my shoulders broaden, I gain lean muscle mass and develop a huge Adam's apple. My saggy man boobs start to morph into a more muscular pectoral shape. Looking in the mirror, I'm becoming a man in front of my own eyes. You could not wipe the smile off my face.

I'm finally normal again and everything is going to be okay, I think.

I feel like I've won the lottery. Now I can fool everyone into thinking I'm just another run-of-the-mill straight boy obsessed with footy and surfing.

If I have a deep voice and facial hair, no one's going to think I'm gay. Right?

I've spent my entire life in Newcastle, the harbour city at the mouth of the Hunter River in New South Wales. There's a lot of energy in Newie, as us locals call it. The city is only a couple of hours north of Sydney, but it has a distinct, down-to-earth vibe all its own.

Newcastle has the largest coal port in the world so it's an industrial town, with thousands of people working in mining and coal. The city is therefore very macho and rough.

This macho ideal goes hand in hand with the infamous drinking scene in Newie. It seems like everyone loves to drink and going for a beer down the pub with your mates is a daily part of life for most men. And the drunker you get and the more of a mess you become, the more people think you're a hero and a legend. Even as a kid, you notice alcohol is always around, at

Christmas parties, holidays and weekend sport.

I don't know what to make of all this. I'm the opposite of everything my city seems to stand for so I feel like I don't have anything of interest or value to offer the people around me. I don't know of one gay person, there are no gay bars and no happily married (or even unhappily married) gay couples. The pressure to fit the macho mould is intense. The rugged ideal Newie man is always looming over me.

I attend The Hunter School of The Performing Arts in Newcastle (HSPA), which is like the school in *Fame* the musical. Every one of the students has stars in their eyes and in a weird way the main thing we all have in common is we are all outcasts just desperate to be heard, seen, and loved. I think Mum encouraged me to go here because she knows I love to dance, do drama, and perform. Also, I think deep down she knows I wouldn't cope at my local high school, which has a reputation for being very rough.

Although I am a lot more accepted at high school than primary school I am definitely still not exactly popular. My favourite subject is drama because I can just let loose and be as silly and outrageous as I want. School itself is somewhat of an escape but seeing as though the majority of my fellow students travelled long distances to attend this school, it means I have zero friends who live locally. I still try my hardest to fit in. The quickest way to become an outcast in this town is by not supporting the Newcastle Knights, the local rugby league team. Rugby league is the game of champions in Newie and the Newcastle Knights are gods walking among us. Every Friday night my family sits on our well-worn couch with fish and chips to cheer the Knights on to victory. Dad, always with an ice-cold beer in hand, and my brothers Ben and Trent discuss individual players' strengths and weaknesses. I try to keep up but can't help but be distracted and fascinated by what's on the screen. Here are these athletic men, wrestling around with each other in a sweaty, muddy writhing mass of muscles, testosterone and sexy footy shorts.

The older I get, the more I look forward to Friday night, when I can admire these mesmerising athletes radiating masculine strength and power. Even though I feel guilty, my balls tingle with excitement. While my dad and brothers cheer their favourite players on, I have to frantically look for cushions on the couch to hide my raging boner. Our desires could not be more different. My brothers want to bang the captain of the cheerleading team and I want to bang the captain of the rugby team. But I play up my sexual attraction to the cheerleaders, no matter how lame my compliments are. This is a secret I must keep at all costs.

A telltale sign I'm in the beginning of puberty – as if I need further proof – is that I'm having a ludicrous number of wet dreams each week. Don't even get me started on how frustrating they are. Every night I dream of having sex with men and wake up with a load of cum all through my bed. It confuses the hell out of me and also fills me with immense fear, even though I know it's only happening in my dreams and nobody will ever find out.

Over time I actually learn to love these wet dreams. Even though the clean-up is messy, the few moments of what feels like real, immersive sex with a man make it all worth it.

I feel like I'm at a turning point in my life. I've always had a sense that I'm not like all the other boys at school, but now it's obvious that I'm attracted to males, and not just on TV during Friday-night football. While most of the other boys my age are looking at girls in the schoolyard, I'm more attracted to certain boys.

It is incredibly confusing and scary to be thinking about the complete opposite of what society tells me I should be thinking about. I'm constantly asking myself, *Why do I prefer how a boy looks over a girl? Why do I continually catch myself daydreaming about the popular boy at school instead of the queen bee?* Then I become terrified that I can't control myself, or I force myself to think about the opposite sex. It's like a never-ending battle in my mind.

My daydreams about men only grow stronger and more frequent. They're becoming a regular part of my daily life. I catch myself appreciating the way a strong male figure looks in movies. Male underwear commercials distract me and I find myself obsessing over the male model on the front of a *Men's Health* magazine.

I'm even beginning to obsess over my brothers' friends. I am way too nervous to hold a conversation with any of them so I just sit and stare, daydreaming about a day when I could possibly be courageous enough to tell someone, anyone, about these feelings I'm having. I'm dying to come clean but I genuinely believe if I'm honest with my brothers' friends or kids at school, I'll get bashed.

Still, I get so excited when my brothers bring their mates over to the house and I try my hardest not to get caught looking at them with my puppy-dog eyes. They're all part of the local rugby league club and one of my favourite things to do on weekends is to go and watch my brothers play football. By which I mean watching their friends tackle each other in footy shorts.

My brother Ben is the captain of his rugby team, so our family almost always gets VIP access to the locker room at the end of each game. This is more exciting than a backstage pass to a Britney Spears concert. The first time I walk into the locker room after the game to congratulate Ben on his win, I am shell-shocked. Here's the entire rugby league team with their shirts off, high-fiving each other in a hot sweaty testosterone fog of masculinity. This intoxicating smell of men's deodorant, mud and perspiration fills the air. The floor is a sea of jerseys, shorts and shoes, and underwear hangs from every hook. Steam billows out of the open showers. I'm the leprechaun who has just found the pot of gold at the end of the steamy rainbow.

As my dad congratulates Ben, I look across to the cloud of steam on the other side of the locker room and try to subtly make out the blurred figures behind it. This is the first time I have come face to face with a sexual fantasy in real life. As the steam begins

28

to disappear, I can see one of the naked figures in the shower: my brother's best friend, who I've always admired from a distance. The air clears, revealing this dripping wet, chiselled god. Then this naked man who looks like he's stepped straight out of my wet dreams begins walking towards me. I gulp.

In a state of panic, I glance away, but this is too good to miss. Forcing myself to be calm, I dart my eyes back. I know this moment in time will provide me with years of masturbation material and it would be a complete crime against humanity to miss it. My heart races, my throat's dry – and I realise I'm getting way too aroused. *Think of something gross before you get an erection!* I scream to myself. I try to picture a vagina in my head and after about thirty seconds I'm able to quickly remove myself from the locker room.

As I jump back into the family car, I can't believe how lucky I've just been. I still have no idea what's happening to me, but I feel excited, liberated and alive. We drive away from the oval, and I decide then and there that I will always be the first to put up my hand to go and congratulate the team in the locker room after each game.

Puberty is proving to be a double-edged sword. It provides me with a man-shaped disguise to hide my sexuality, but it's opened a Pandora's box in terms of my sexual desires and feelings for men. I try my hardest to think about women and to appreciate a woman's body but inevitably seconds later catch myself googling 'Men's Health Magazine Cover' on the computer.

One afternoon I'm home alone and decide to jump onto the computer and search for some male-on-male pornography. I had watched straight porn but only paid attention to the man and knew what I really desired was to see porn with only men. I type 'GAY PORN' and then my finger trembles as it hovers over the search bar. I take a deep breath and hit Search, knowing there is no turning back. I'm terrified of the potential repercussions if I'm caught but the thrill is just irresistible.

I've struck gold. I'm bombarded with page after page of gay pornography. Finally, the things I've been imagining in my head are right in front of me. I no longer have to just settle for a man in footy shorts on TV but now have a bare arse and a penis staring back at me. Instead of looking at a guy with his shirt off, now I'm watching two men totally naked and having sex.

Visualising myself in this scene, on my knees giving pleasure to this sexy man, my hand automatically goes down my pants and I feel myself about to ejaculate within seconds.

All my senses are on high alert as I listen out for any family members' cars pulling up in the driveway or a neighbour knocking on the front door. The house is empty and silent, but my heart is thumping. And then —

I have officially climaxed for the first time awake and watching gay porn.

Seconds later a wave of guilt washes over me. My entire body starts trembling and I feel myself go pale. What have I done?! The thoughts in my head can never be seen but this search history definitely can. I need to erase my deep dark secret from the world, and I need to do it *fast*.

I sit at the computer for the next ten minutes trying to delete the history. I decide to search for 'STRAIGHT PORN' on the off-chance that, if I'm caught, at least it will be for straight porn. Which is nowhere near as bad, right?

I've been taught that I should desire women, have a girlfriend, and then one day marry a woman and have kids. That is the complete opposite of what I want in life. The hardest part about it is there is no one in my life or even in movies or on television that has what I so desperately want in my head. I don't have anyone to relate to and feel so lost and alone in the world. I can't connect with anyone and don't know who to turn to for help or advice. And as much as I want guidance and support there is no way in hell I have the courage to be truthful about my feelings.

I try to escape reality by disappearing into TV shows. Our Foxtel box seems like my only friend some days, and I watch *Simpsons* marathons, endless makeover shows, music videos and mindless cartoons to take my mind of my inner struggles.

Sometimes I lock myself in my room and re-create scenes from my favourite TV shows and movies to pass the time (like *Harry Potter* re-enactments, but I always cast myself as Hermione Granger). I claimed the family's clunky, old-school video camera and make my own silly little home videos all by myself. I feel like

I can be as silly and outrageous as I like in them, but I never let anyone see them once I finish because I am way too embarrassed.

But no matter how hard I try to distract myself, there is always a sense of worry and anxiety about what is to come – a feeling that's just growing stronger and stronger.

In the background, all's not well at home. After Dad's accident, his physical health deteriorates and he's forced to leave his job as a builder. This puts a lot of pressure and stress on my parents' marriage, and they're always bickering. My brothers and I are often walking on eggshells just waiting for the next argument. This has become the norm. Something has to give.

We go on a family trip to our holiday home in Port Stephens, about an hour's drive north of Newcastle. While we're there, Mum and Dad sit my brothers and me down and explain that they are separating, and that Dad will begin living at the holiday house for good.

'We both love you boys with all our hearts; however, we know our family unit will be stronger and happier if we go our separate ways,' Mum says, as we all sob on the couch together. And then we just go home without Dad.

From that point onwards there's actually more harmony in our lives. My parents get along and are very friendly and amicable with each other.

4

ROD: 'Dear God, please heal me'

Dear God, I'm so sorry I am this way, I don't want to be this way. I hate myself and feel so dirty. I beg of you God, please heal me, I don't want to be like this. I promise if you heal me, I'll do whatever you ask. Please God, please.

When I was younger these 'if you do this for me, then I will do this for you' conversations with God were simpler. I'd ask for the latest Pokémon cards, for the sun to be out for my birthday party or for no one to find the pot plant I smashed playing footy.

Now there's only one thing that I ever ask God for. In fact, I don't ask; I plead, I beg. I go to bed every night, pull the blankets over my head and cry out to God for this one simple thing.

Every night I cry until my throat hurts and my eyes are so sore that I can't keep them open and I cry myself to sleep. The pain is so much worse than any physical pain I have ever felt.

In daylight hours, I'm putting up a good front. I'm in the popular group at school and I'm known as the guy who always has a girlfriend. I'm getting good grades, I'm fit and play basketball, tennis and soccer. Pretty perfect for a teenager, you'd think.

I'm the standout good Christian student leader. I'm involved in a lunchtime program called United, where we preach from the Bible, sing songs of worship and pray for each other. I also help to organise Prayer and Praise, a compulsory weekly subject where a band plays and a preacher speaks to the school. I even want to be a pastor.

Around me, life as I know it is rapidly changing. No longer do us boys talk about Pokémon and Dragon Ball Z and other childish cartoons; we talk about girls, boobs, pubes, boners, porn and wanking, just to name a few topics. We no longer play hide and seek or tag anymore; now it's fun to do nudie runs, dack your mates, and hand out arse slaps and sack-whacks.

I allow people in my life to see this cool, calm and confident boy; no one would ever guess the torment I'm living with every day. It seems to me that as time goes on my 'admiration' towards men is transforming into something else, something stronger until there's no point trying to deny it: I'm attracted to men.

I'm noticing them more. I like facial hair, deep voices and muscles. I'm so confused about why I'm becoming attracted to male teachers at school and my male friends. I'm supposed to be looking at the girls at school who roll up their skirts to make them miniskirts and checking out the ones who undo too many buttons on their blouse to show a bit of cleavage but no, here I am looking at my male PE teacher's ass after he decides to wear shorts one size too small. I am losing my mind.

My friends have all discovered masturbation and like to brag about it. Some even steal their older brothers' porn magazines and we all go to our after-school hangout and take a look … I hope nobody notices that I always stare at the male in the image; the female may as well not be there. I don't find vaginas attractive in the least.

I masturbate virtually every time I have a shower. I close my eyes and fantasise about men (from friends or teachers to celebrities and sport stars) I always feel bad about it afterwards but that doesn't mean I don't do it again the next day. Later I tell my friends about it – just leaving out the little detail of who I was masturbating over.

One weekend I have the house to myself and work up the courage to use the family computer to look up porn. I walk from one end of the house to the other yelling, 'Hello, is anyone home?' just to double check.

I turn on the computer and after what feels like a lifetime of waiting for the dial-up internet to connect, I open Google and type 'Hot Porn' then click on the first webpage that comes up. My heart is pumping so fast; this is the naughtiest thing I have ever done.

Looking at the home page of this site, my eyes are drawn to a tab called 'Categories'. *What could this be?* I nervously click it. The word 'gay' leaps out at me. I can't resist. My palms are sweaty but I click the tab. The stupid dial-up internet is torturously slow to load.

But it pays off. My computer screen fills up with men doing stuff with other men. I furiously click on everything I can find for the next half an hour. I've always been taught that 'homosexuality is an abomination', but what I'm looking at feels right in every way. I feel a strange sense of acceptance. For the first time I don't hate myself for feeling the way I do.

There's this one video I keep watching over and over again – mainly because it's one of the few that fully loads. These fit, muscly dudes are in wrestling outfits ready to fight in a boxing arena. There's a referee and everything. The referee blows his whistle to start the fight and these two masculine men start wrestling on the ground, pulling each other's outfits off and slapping each other's arses, until they are fully naked, fondling each other and eventually having sex. I can't help fantasising about some of the older popular guys at school who I would not mind wrestling like this with. I feel like I'm in Gay Disneyland.

Then I hear the sound of the garage door opening.

Shit!

Someone's home.

My heart stops. I want to be sick.

Here I am, sitting in front of the computer absolutely butt naked with the biggest erection I have ever had, seconds away from relieving myself. Frantically I start closing the computer windows. *Shit shit shit, Rod, how many pages did you open?* I finish shutting them and quickly turn the computer screen off. I hear the door from the garage open and Dad shouts, 'Hello!' I race to the bathroom and turn the shower on so Dad will just think I didn't hear him.

The shower runs but I don't get in. Instead I sit on the cold bathroom tiles, up against the bath, rocking back and forth sweating and crying, barely able to breathe.

It passes. I catch my breath, get myself off the floor and jump in the shower, with an erection that hasn't gone away. I close my eyes and as the water washes over my body the images of the wrestlers appear in my head, and I'm done in ten seconds.

That was so disgusting. What's wrong with me?

Self-hatred creeps in and despite the shower I feel a dirtiness I've never felt before.

I skip dinner and tell my parents I'm not feeling well. I go straight to bed and yet again try to make a deal with God:

Dear God, heal me from this. When I wake up, I want to be STRAIGHT!

The next day, I get up as though nothing is wrong. I've become extremely good at hiding what's really going on inside my head so I almost believe nothing *is* wrong. I pack my school bag and walk to the bus stop for school like the good Christian boy I am. I put on a smile, help to organise United, sit with my current girlfriend, Rachel, at lunch and hold her hand. But all I can think about is what happened yesterday afternoon.

After school the bus drops me at the end of the street and as I walk down the path towards my house, I get a sick feeling in my stomach. I walk through the front door and into the kitchen where Mum is sipping her cup of tea. She always has a certain look on her face when she's not happy and she certainly has that look now. 'Go put your bag in your room,' she says, 'and see your father, he wants to talk to you.'

My heart sinks; I feel like I could either throw up or faint … *Please let it be faint so I can avoid this.*

The walk down the hall to my room at the back of the house seems to take an eternity. As I dump my bag I know exactly what Dad wants to talk to me about.

I didn't delete my browsing history. I did not have time. It all happened so fast.

I walk back past Mum, through the kitchen and into the lounge room where Dad is sitting at the end of the three-seater lounge waiting for me. I sit down at the other end and look at him. He doesn't look back at me, but I can see his eyes are watery.

'Rod, I found something on the computer that made me feel sick,' he says.

Silence. *Think, Rod, think. Try to think of an excuse.*

Dad continues, 'There was men having sex with other men. You're not Gay, are you?'

'No,' I quickly reply. My hands are shaking and I just want to cry. 'I was on the internet and these pop-ups came up and I didn't know what they were, so I clicked on them.' I ramble on, trying to talk my way out of it. 'When I realised what it was, I only looked out of curiosity because I didn't even know how two men had sex. I didn't like it, I promise.' I pause. 'It made me feel sick.'

'Okay.' Dad accepts my explanation with no further question.

Just like that. I don't think he's prepared to accept that his son could be Gay. That's not the life he wants for me, so it's easier for him to brush it aside and hope I'm telling the truth.

So I'm off the hook. But, from that day on, I can feel myself spiralling downwards. On the outside, things go on as normal. Mum packs me lunch every day: a Vegemite sandwich, a donut and a small packet of chips. I don't want to eat my lunches and throw them away when I get to school. I still eat when Mum is around so no one will suspect anything is wrong. I don't like who I am inside and hate the person I see looking back in the mirror. Food is one thing I can control and hide very well.

Where I used to see light all I start to see is darkness. I'm stuck in an unhealthy pattern of fantasising about men, enjoying it, then feeling incredibly guilty and dirty afterwards, and skipping meals. It's also a distraction because forcing myself to go hungry makes me think of food as opposed to how much of a disgrace I am.

Night after night I lie in bed, crying out to God to take it away. He never does.

One night it dawns on me that I am never going to be healed. I've tried everything, and I'm in so much pain. I get out of bed, open up my school bag, find my pencil case and pull out my scissors. I remove my watch, throw the blankets over my head and with tears dripping onto the sheets in front of me, I place the blade on my wrist and apply just enough pressure to break my skin and cut myself. The pain distracts me from the torture going on inside my head, but otherwise doesn't help. If anything, it gives me something else to feel guilty about and one more thing to hide.

One day Mum gives me her old phone after she buys a new one. I can browse the internet on it. It's even slower than on the family computer but at least I can look at what I desire in the privacy of my own room at night, without the fear of getting caught. Every time I look at gay porn I thoroughly enjoy it. Then I hate myself for enjoying it, and feel guilt ridden. But I do this over and over. Mum keeps asking how I go through my credit so quickly, and I tell her I must've pocket-dialled someone.

At school, my favourite teacher asks me if I want to preach in front of my peers at Prayer and Praise about 'The power of words and how they affect people'. She tells me that I will need to do it twice, once in front of middle school and again for high school. I agree in order to keep up my strong, good-Christian-boy image, but my stomach does backflips.

The day of my talk arrives. Walking to the front I feel my guts clench, but speaking in front of people is something I'm good at and I manage to project confidence. I notice my mum beaming proudly at the back of the room. She is standing next to my youth pastor, who has just started at the Baptist Church I'm attending. The hall is packed with about three hundred of my peers, and I feel like everyone is watching me, hanging on my every word.

I begin by telling them that I once was confused and 'maybe' thought I was Gay. 'I gave my struggle over to God, knowing he is all-powerful and comes to the aid of the weak.' So far so true. I do pray that God will take the gay away; it just doesn't work.

But then I deliver what everyone wants to hear: 'I put all my trust in him and he looked into my heart and healed me. He has healed me from those lies from the Devil and I feel free.'

I wrap up my message by offering for anyone who is believing lies from the devil to come down the front so that I can pray for them, and they can feel the freedom I feel. The room goes silent and my heart beats super fast. *Have I just exposed myself for having even had these thoughts? Am I the only one who's struggled with this?*

A guy from the year below me stands and walks to the front. He whispers to me, 'Everyone always calls me gay too. Can you pray for me?' I close my eyes and pray over him and then give him a hug. As I open my eyes there are about twenty other people who have come to the front, boys and girls from all different years.

I pray for a lot of people but as Prayer and Praise ends I am filled with shame. I'm a total fraud. What makes it even worse is that the first guy who came to the front asks me to be his mentor so I can help him with all the negative thoughts he is having, because he thinks I have beat them.

5

ROD: Halfway out

There's one good thing about attending a Christian school: it's incredibly easy for me to hide my true feelings – or lack thereof – about girls. Sex before marriage is a sin so there's no pressure to have a sexual relationship with a girl. At the same time, I'm popular, so finding girlfriends is no problem and gives me the perfect cover.

It seems as though I've had a new girlfriend every term since I started at this school in Year 6, from the queen of the cool girls to one of the nerdy girls I've become besties with to the girl who could sing like an angel. I just always have to be in a relationship as cover. Mum asks me, 'Who's your girlfriend this week?' and most of the time the name's changed since she last asked me. I have the nickname 'Bicycle' at school because I've gone around every girl in our year and even dated girls in the years above us. I figure, if I commit myself to a set path, pray hard and 'date' the right girls – or all the girls – then no one will ever know my secret.

There are many issues that come from this. I feel terrible about it for a start. And no matter how hard I try, I can't ignore the ever-present desires that linger in my mind. Plus I'm in Year 10; will I be able to keep up this pretence once I leave?

As it turns out, when I head into Year 11 it becomes apparent that school is no longer for me. In the first few weeks of term I score a prefect badge, but I'm really not a studier and don't want another two years of it. I decide it's time to drop out and start a new life.

In a classic parental reaction, Mum and Dad declare I have two options: work or a different kind of study. I choose work. I've been working at a local supermarket and they're very happy to give me more hours. I want to please my parents so I set my sights on a more permanent position at work.

More importantly, I'm determined to pursue a life that pleases God. I need to do something or be someone who makes my parents and my God proud. This 'being into boys' thing certainly doesn't fit the plan. A huge part of me still believes that it could just be a phase and if I do enough good deeds to please God then maybe, just maybe, after all these years he will heal me. The other part of me is stressed out of my mind and hopes that if I can stay in my parents' good books and be the son they've always hoped for and think they have, then they may not take it as hard when (if!) I share my true self with them.

Boom! The perfect idea hits me: I'm going to enrol in Bible college in Sydney. I sit in church all the time and hear about this college, where lots of young Christian leaders go to learn more about the Bible and get their credentials to become pastors. I'm so involved in my church and Christian activities that this feels like a natural path and one that will sit well with my parents and surely get me some brownie points with God. I think this is my calling from God to study the Bible and become a pastor like the leaders in church are always preaching. The only voice I can hear in my head is mine, but I'm willing to roll with this. Surely if I choose this path, I can't be Gay – God has to fix me!

I sit Mum and Dad down. They have these worried looks on their faces. I don't blame them; last time there was a sit-down, Dad had found gay porn on the family computer.

This time it's different. 'I've been praying and I feel that I'm being called by God to enrol in Bible college in Sydney,' I say.

From the huge smile on Mum's face, I can tell she's so proud of me, which makes me feel great … but at the same time like a complete fraud.

'Start taking steps towards this and if it's meant to be then God will open the door,' she says, giving me a big hug.

Almost immediately I find an incredible place to stay, hosted by a Christian family doing their bit to support the Church. Mum, Dad and I decide to take the two-hour drive from Newcastle to Sydney's Northern Beaches to check out their house. We drive into this estate that has the biggest, most modern and luxurious houses I have ever seen. We park the car in a gorgeous tree-lined street, walk past the brand-new BMW and Mercedes sitting in the driveway and up to the oversized front door. Through the glass I can see an enormous Cinderella staircase. I knock on the door and we're greeted by a beautiful young couple and their toddler. They show us around. We walk up the Cinderella stairs into the main living room and kitchen area, which looks out over the pool and then onto a spectacular view of the valley. They even point out the church complex where Bible college will be. They then walk us downstairs, where there's a small lounge room with a TV and beanbags, a big desk in the corner, a bathroom and a room with a queen bed. They tell me this whole floor of their beautiful mansion in Sydney's northern beaches is mine to rent if I want it.

'I'll take it,' I immediately say.

As he drives us back to Newcastle Dad asks me, 'Are you 100 per cent sure about this, mate?'

I don't even have to say anything, because Mum says, 'You wouldn't understand this but Rod listens to God when he speaks and this is what he's been called to do.' Dad isn't a Christian, but he loves Mum so much and would do practically anything to make her happy.

Dad darts a look at Mum, and then catches my eye in the rear-view mirror.

'Well then, we're happy to support you financially over the next couple of years while you're here,' he says.

That's thousands of dollars of college fees, as well as rent. I'm blown away.

'Thank you,' I say. It seems inadequate but I think they can tell how grateful I am.

As soon as we get home, I tee up a meeting at work and go speak to my manager about getting a transfer to a store closer to college. There's no way I'm driving two hours to and from work every day and doing college as well. My manager makes a few calls to HR and just like that my transfer is complete; all I need to do is give them a start date. If that's not a sign that I'm doing the right thing, then nothing is. Mum said to start making steps towards this to see if God will open the door and it looks like doors are opening.

So why do I feel like this is a mistake? Everything is pointing to 'YES, do it!', but something inside is screaming *NO, don't do it!* I'm trying as hard as I possibly can to make the right choices, to follow the right path and please everyone. It's as though I'm making all the right moves but heading towards what I know in my heart is the wrong destination.

The deposit is paid for college and for my boujee mansion. I'm all set to move in just under two weeks. But I keep lying in bed at night, wide awake, fighting with myself.

I feel so frustrated with what I've done but I'm coming to the realisation that Bible college is the last thing I want to do. This sets off a flurry of questions: *What happens if I pull out? Will Dad lose his deposits? Will I still have a job at the supermarket? What will I tell my parents?*

After yet another sleepless night I again ask my parents if I can talk to them. We sit down on the same lounge where all our serious talks seem to happen. I feel sick.

'I've been thinking a lot,' I start, and Mum and Dad look at each other in confusion. 'I know God has called me to Bible college but the more I pray and the more I think about it, I don't think the timing is right.' Silence fills the room, my heart skips a beat, Mum and Dad continue to look puzzled. Before they have a chance to respond, I explain, 'I'll definitely re-enrol down the track, I just don't feel comfortable being so financially reliant on you.'

Dad is the first to speak. I actually think he's happy. 'Well mate, I think that's wise and you can always do it later if you want. I'd much prefer you knuckle down, save some money and buy a house.'

I nod in agreement.

But Mum says, 'This is what God has called you to do, Rod, you told us that. I honestly believe this is the Devil lying to you, trying to stop you doing what God wants.'

I don't know what to say. In the end I just repeat, 'Sorry, Mum, I'm just not comfortable with you supporting me.'

She's obviously so disappointed, but nods her head.

Dad says, 'Mate, we love you very much and we'll support you whatever decision you make.'

While they tell me it's my decision, I can see Mum's shattered. And I've lost some of Dad's money, so I agree to pay him back.

At least I've bought myself some time.

With my adjusted plans semi in place, I score myself a full-time job working at a travel agency, the same company my sister

Emma works for, just a different location. Other than the owners, there are zero other men working for the company. Travel's a very female- and gay-man-dominated industry. This should be great for me, but it's really not going to help me hide. Every person who comes into my store or walks past will automatically assume I'm that way inclined. My only hope is to devote myself to God, attend church each week and lead youth group on Friday nights.

My attraction towards men, however, is not going away; in fact, it's growing every day. The more I try to convince myself it's not real but just lies from the Devil and, as importantly, persuade the people in my life that I'm not gay, the stronger the thoughts become.

I need to talk to someone. *Who can I trust? Who can I pour my heart out to without getting into trouble or being ridiculed?*

Dean is in his mid-twenties. I meet him through a mutual friend at church. I see Dean around a lot and he seems fun to hang out with, has a really cool job working for a charity organisation and I feel comfortable around him. I look up to him as somewhat of a mentor. I wonder whether I can confide in him.

I'm nervous about asking Dean to hang out one on one; I'm only sixteen and can't even drive yet. Regardless, I sum up the courage to ask him. Dean doesn't seem at all uncomfortable about it and replies, 'How 'bout I pick you up and we can go for a drive?'

Mum and Dad know of Dean from church so have no issues with me hanging out with an older guy. It's a spectacular day. When he arrives at my parents' house I walk down the driveway to meet him. He's sitting in his car and looks right at me with a big grin on his face. I can't help but smile back. I open the car door and he smells so good, like he's just covered himself in cologne. He asks me what I want to do, and I suggest we just go park down by the lake not far from the house and go for a walk.

The sun is shining and the lake looks like glass; it's kind of romantic. We park the car and start walking, making small talk.

Then Dean asks me, 'Why did you want to hang out?'

It catches me off guard and I try to come up with something believable. 'A lot of my friends are still in school; I want to make some older friends and I like you.'

He looks me dead in the eye with that same smirk from the car and says, 'I like you too.'

I feel my face go red and my heart rate increase. I can't believe I'm blushing; I hope he doesn't notice. I'm feeling a spark like I've never really had with a man before. I always admire from afar and like what I see – but blushing and getting butterflies in my stomach? This is new.

As we continue our walk, laughing and having a good time, we come up to a park bench. Dean asks me to sit down. He looks nervous and says, 'I want to ask you something, but you can't tell anyone what I'm about to say.'

'Of course,' I reply.

He looks at me, then looks away. When he looks back he hesitates, then asks, 'Have you ever done anything with a guy?'

I know exactly what he's implying but respond, 'What do you mean?'

He asks me for reassurance that what he's about to tell me won't go any further. He explains that, for a long time now, he has felt this attraction towards men and really has no interest in women at all. I listen closely to everything he says and with every word I feel this sense of relief.

I am not alone.

Dean pours his heart out, telling me about how hard it's been for him having Christian parents, growing up in the Church, being a Christian himself, attending a Christian school and having Christian friends. He looks intently at me and takes a big breath. 'Pretty much, I think I'm Gay.'

My eyes start to well up and I feel a closeness to Dean unlike anything I've felt before – like we've been best friends for years and now I know his deepest darkest secret.

I pause and then say, 'It's okay, I won't tell anyone.'

'Oh gee, thanks,' he laughs.

I smile up at him, nervous as hell.

'I know exactly how you feel,' I tell him, struggling to make eye contact.

For the next hour or so we talk and we talk and we talk. I share all my attractions to the guys at school and my hot school teacher, I tell him about my struggles at night and the severe anxiety I face each day, I tell him about my failed attempt to enrol in Bible college and how much my feelings about guys scare the shit out of me.

We've both been fighting the same battles. It's such a comfort to know that there are others just like me.

When Dean drops me home, we vow this will be our secret and agree to catch up again very soon.

How incredible to have found someone I feel so free with; it's as if I don't have to hide anymore.

As I go to bed, I feel at ease for the first time in years. I can't stop thinking about Dean. Just as I'm falling asleep, my phone buzzes and a text from Dean pops up on my screen: 'Goodnight Stud xx.' *Did he just call me stud and send me kisses?* I think to myself as I roll over and go to sleep, feeling excited about seeing Dean again.

We text all week, sharing more little secrets and signing off every message with an 'X'. Dean encourages me to save his number under a girl's name in case anyone sees it.

On Friday he asks me if I want to hang out again, this time at his place. I take a little while to reply as I think I know what he's hinting at and I'm not sure if I'm at the point of experimenting sexually. But I end up saying, 'Yeah sure.' He tells me he'll come pick me up the next day.

I'm up early on Saturday morning, feeling nervous about going to Dean's house. Mum comes into the kitchen while I'm eating breakfast and asks me what my plans are for the day.

'Just hanging out with Dean again,' I calmly reply.

Mum is delighted. Both of my parents actively encourage his 'mentorship' as my 'good Christian role model', which I guess is the upside to finding a guy within the Church to talk to.

In the afternoon Dean texts me to tell me he's on his way. I get this intense thrill. I don't know if it's this further validation that he likes me, the anticipation of what could happen or just the fact I don't have to hide around Dean.

Along with the excitement, arousal and anticipation come nerves. I'm so unprepared; I'm still not 100 per cent sure I want something to happen. The only knowledge I have of gay sex is what I've seen in porn. My school's sex education program consisted of a 'no sex till marriage' mantra and I don't have a single person I can ask, not that I'd be brave enough anyway.

I have the longest shower in history. When I get out I decide it's now or never. Freshly washed, lathered and spritzed, I throw on my favourite pair of Calvin Klein underwear, just in case he sees them. He arrives outside, I say bye to Mum and head out the front.

When I get in the car Dean says, 'Wow, you smell great.' I smile and feel instantly at ease.

'Thanks,' I say as I settle in. His car also smells good, just like it did the last time we hung out.

'You also look so sexy,' he adds, glancing over at me. I can feel myself blushing. I was thinking the same thing about him. The conversation continues to be very flirty on the drive to Dean's.

He asks me if I've ever kissed a guy or gone any further. He keeps telling me how sexy I look and grabbing my thigh as he drives. My hands are on my lap, trying to conceal the huge erection he's giving me. Thank God I'm wearing tight skinny jeans.

When we get back to his place, a small unit at the back of another house, I follow him inside and he shows me around. He asks if I want a drink or anything to eat. I'm way too nervous to eat anything so I say no thanks.

'Let's go chill in my room,' he says, and seconds later we're heading down the hallway. The air is thick with men's deodorant – perhaps Dean has prepped for this as much as I have? We walk into his room and I sit down on the bed; my heart is racing. I keep asking him if anyone is due home as I'm starting to anticipate what could happen next. After he reassures me for perhaps the tenth time that we're alone, he tells me to move up closer to him. My heart beats even faster, and my breath gets even shorter; I think he can tell how nervous I am. I shuffle up the bed but am far too nervous to make eye contact. I can feel a strange grin on my face, which I can't help getting whenever I'm around Dean.

'What's funny?' he asks.

I just giggle and say, 'Nothing, I don't know why I'm laughing.'

We're right next to each other, leaning against the bedhead. After an awkward pause, which I can only assume is him getting up his nerve, he leans over and kisses me. At first I'm shocked by his facial hair and the immediate tongue in my mouth. *This is a guy.* I panic and pull away feeling like I've ruined the moment.

'It's okay,' Dean says. 'You don't have to do anything you don't want to.'

We lie there just cuddling for a bit until I tell him I want to try again and, hoping to redeem myself, lean in for another kiss.

This time it feels right.

I've never felt so normal as in this moment. The connection I have with Dean is beyond labels and beyond words. Right now, the world has stopped, and we are the only two people who matter.

It's not like I expected: it's way better. Dean rolls onto me and I wrap my legs around him. His muscular, manly body on top of me feels so right and I forget about everything else. There's no fear of judgement, no shame, no consequences, just the two of us following our instincts.

We lie there kissing for ages, feeling each other's bodies; we take each other's clothes off and run our hands all over each other. We go down on each other, and I can tell Dean wants to take it one step further. He keeps trying to put his finger inside me, but I keep telling him I'm not ready, even though I'm so curious. *What would it feel like to have him inside me?* My only knowledge of the gay world is from porn and that doesn't exactly come with a how-to guide. I'm partly scared anal sex will hurt but more worried about the potential 'dirty' consequences. The possible embarrassment is more than I can take, and I'm not ready for that. I keep thinking, *If I do this, then that makes me gay*, which is ridiculous but, in this moment, feels all too real.

Dean is such a gentleman; he doesn't push the issue and we get each other off in the most magical way. I have never felt this close to another person before and no one has ever made me feel such pleasure. It's so much better than watching porn alone under my blankets every night.

On the drive home I'm really quiet. Part of me feels liberated and like I just became a man; the other part is riddled with guilt.

Dean and I keep hooking up secretly. But I'm still set on not having actual penetrative sex because to me there is no going back from that. Also, from the few times I've experimented with myself, I just don't know if I want a penis inside of me.

We attend church conferences together and present as upstanding men of God doing great things for the Church. Little does anybody know what we're getting up to after church and that both of us are living what feels like a double life.

When I'm with Dean it feels right. I can switch off from my crippling anxiety and just enjoy being in his company.

Then immediately after I leave Dean's side and I'm alone, I hate myself. I feel dirty, as though I've just committed a terrible crime. In bed at night I feel a sense of calm when Dean and I are texting but the second he says goodnight, my negative thoughts come rushing back.

Turning seventeen feels like a pivotal moment, like I've stepped into manhood. I get my driver's licence, which means I can come and go as I please and don't need to explain myself to anyone, which feels great and very freeing.

More importantly, I am now 100 per cent certain that I like boys – and that I need to tell people, to stop living a lie. Maybe it's because I can't handle the pressure of the guilt anymore; maybe I need to live in the open. I decide to tell another friend from church, Heath, the one who introduced me to Dean in the first place. At the end of the day, I haven't had penetrative sex so I can't be completely gay, right?

Dean knows something is up. I stop replying to text messages so much and when I do, my answers are short. He asks me, 'Are you okay?' and I always just reply, 'Yep, I'm fine.'

When I finally confess things to Heath, he stays pretty calm and doesn't show much emotion at all, which makes me feel comfortable. I feel a weight lift. Then he tells me that he isn't angry with me, which is what I've been so afraid of, but that he's disappointed in Dean.

My positive feeling quickly turns to panic and anxiety. I hadn't considered our age gap at all; I was so caught up in my own thoughts and desire to make myself feel better than I hadn't even thought about this.

When I arrive home at the end of the day my parents are sitting together in the lounge room (I am beginning to hate this bloody lounge room). They are clearly waiting to talk to me. They both look agitated and my dad is enraged. Heath felt he was obliged to share everything I just confessed to him with the youth pastor – and, as I'm technically underage, the Church felt they had a moral responsibility to intervene and called my parents.

Emotions are running high. I don't think I've ever seen my dad so mad. Ever since he found the gay porn on the computer a couple of years earlier, I've felt he was suspicious of me but just couldn't let himself believe that his son was gay. Dad's response is a combination of his worst nightmare coming true and the sense, fuelled by the Church, that I had been taken advantage of.

'Where does the mongrel live? I am going to knock his block off,' Dad yells.

'We really need to press charges, we need to let the police know,' says Mum. 'He has sexually abused you Rod, that's not okay,' she cries. Mum cries.

They both keep asking if I'm okay. They keep telling me I've been taken advantage of and sexually abused by Dean. They tell me what I feel towards Dean is not real, that he's been messing with my head.

I sob uncontrollably; I feel so bad, for Dean and for myself.

'What have I done wrong?' I manage to ask. 'Is he going to get into trouble?'

My questions go unanswered and my promises of 'I know what I am doing' and 'I'm not a child' fall on deaf ears.

I feel the moment bubbling up. This is it. *I need to tell them.* I am about to share my struggles, my shame, my truth. My thoughts are racing, and I feel panic like nothing I've ever felt before. Some part of me still thinks it could be the Devil lying to me, or a phase I'm going through but that if I admitted to it now no girl would ever want to be with me in the future.

Wait a minute, if I do this there's no going back … Am I even actually gay?

I have it. I'll just tell my parents I'm bisexual, that way they'll still have hope that I'll end up with a girl. At the end of the day, I like girls, right?

'I am bisexual!' I yell.

There's dead silence. I continue, 'I am into girls *and* guys,' as though they don't know what bisexual means. I explain that I have struggled with this for as long as I can remember.

But they are in no position to listen to or accept this information. All they can see is a victim. Someone in need of help. Their not-so-innocent youngest child is confused and hurt.

6

TIM: Sex, drugs and a drunk tank

'Here you go, sir.'

I cannot wipe the grin off my face as I get my boarding pass from the Qantas check-in desk and see my shiny new backpack go backwards on the conveyor belt and out of sight.

I'm going to Canada and I am thrilled! I am also extremely nervous and scared because I'm planning on being away for nearly nine months. My entire family has come to see me off and I am hugging my mum non-stop to make up for all those hugs I'll miss. Dad and my brothers are excited for me but too manly to shed a tear, while Mum and I can't stop crying. They all wave goodbye as I walk through the departure gate. I don't want to walk around the corner and lose sight of them so I just stand there for a moment with tears pouring down my cheeks.

Boarding the plane, it really hits me that I'm doing this adventure all by myself. The other passengers on the plane keep to themselves, ignoring this kid crying in the window seat. It's not until I start listening to my iPod that I can collect myself and start to feel excited again. I make a declaration to myself: I will come back from this trip a man, leaving behind all the pathetic past baggage I hate about myself.

I take advantage of the complimentary booze, and as I knock back drink after drink I refine my goals. *I will have sex with as many girls as possible during my time in Canada. If I am able to have sex with heaps of girls, I will be straight, right?*

This is a new start, for a new me. Coming back home a sexually confused and ashamed virgin is not an option. My mantra from this point on is, 'I will lose my virginity and it will be with a girl.'

High school was a long, hard slog trying to hide who I really was and be like everyone else. By the time I finished Year 12 I was mentally and emotionally exhausted, and the idea of spending a gap year away from it all was just irresistible.

I've always dreamed of spending a big chunk of time abroad and loved the idea of a working holiday where I get to meet new people, throw myself into spontaneous adventures and explore parts of the world I have never been before. Not to mention that on the other side of the world I'll have the freedom to do whatever my heart desires. Somehow, I've never really had that stage in life of rebelling against authority and pushing boundaries. Now is my chance. I feel like a caged eagle about to spread my wings.

As nervous as I am to be travelling to the other side of the world by myself, there's something so exhilarating about leaving everything I know behind. The new people I meet will have no idea about my struggles with my sexuality and identity. I can be whoever I want to be without any preconceived judgement.

Los Angeles is my ultimate destination for this grand new chapter in my life – the glitz and glamour of the Hollywood lifestyle really calls to me. I want so much to be celebrated and loved for who I truly am, and Hollywood seems like the perfect place to make this a reality. All the fierce queens I idolise – Katy Perry, Lady Gaga and Beyoncé – call LA home and I reckon going there will let me be just as strong, empowered and brave as them.

My Hollywood dreaming had become a bit of a fixation, and I'd got a job at an ugg boot shop run by friends of the family so I could save as much money as possible, break free of my city and fly myself to America. I was obsessed with pop culture and desperately wanted to entertain people and have people admire me for just being myself. I was forever daydreaming and would always be off with the fairies fantasising about my Hollywood Hills mansion and name in lights. It got so intense I began consuming copious amounts of coffee to help me work as many shifts at the ugg boot store as possible to fuel my future American fantasy life.

I had researched working holiday opportunities in America for months, but setting up a job over there was a lot harder than it looked, borderline impossible. After a lot of frustration, I found out from a close family friend that it's a lot easier for Australians to get a job in Canada due to the working holiday visa. Immediately, my guard went up. My heart had been set on America for so long and I knew next to nothing about Canada. *Still, it can't hurt to have a look*, I thought. When I did, I fell in love with the natural beauty and Canada became my new destination.

Pristine turquoise lakes sit among the most breathtaking mountain ranges and endless glaciers; I see animals in real life that I've only ever seen in movies. Canada is everything I thought it would be and more! Grizzly bears, moose and wolves are all on my doorstep (sometimes literally) and it feels like every day I'm coming face to face with new wildlife and magnificent, unfamiliar landscapes. I'm in love with the place – this will be the perfect backdrop for the biggest moment of my life.

I have one goal for my working holiday: I'm going to be a rockstar at the biggest Rock Camp of all time. I will live and breathe sex, drugs and rock 'n' roll. I'm going to party like I've never partied before, I don't care if they have to carry me out of Canada on a stretcher straight into rehab. I'm going to have the best time of my life and go back to Australia a straight man with loads of stories about the hundreds of women I've slept with.

My new job is at one of the most prestigious five-star hotels in Banff, a resort town in the province of Albert, located within the Banff National Park and smack-bang in the middle of the majestic Rocky Mountains, which are so big they make me feel like an ant. Banff's dramatic beauty is almost overwhelming; it's a paradise for hikers, horseback riding and rock climbers. The town itself is pristine and the definition of picture perfect, the sort of place where it's virtually impossible to take a bad photograph. The shop fronts are all decorated with bright coloured flowers and Canadian flags hang over the entrance of every pub, café, and restaurant in town. A railway weaves throughout the town and 'Caution: Deer' and 'Bear Crossing' signs about, while an old stone bridge spans the Bow River and joins the main street to the Mountain and the hotel where I'm living and working.

My job is in the events department, helping set up and run functions. Our team is a group of young, fun and outgoing people from Canada and other travellers undertaking the same gap year as myself. In other words, we all love to party.

The hotel is huge and the staff live onsite. I share a room with two other Aussie guys. One of my roommates, Luke, is really sexy, and I get turned on when he is changing or coming in and out of our shower. He is into lifting weights and he's the first guy who motivates me to work out – we often lift weights together in the hotel's gym. The staff are a big group of friends and after work we all hang out together, having drinks in someone's room before hitting the nightclubs.

The biggest character is a Canadian girl called Mandy, and she makes me feel special. She laughs at everything I say, puts me on a 'funny guy' pedestal. I love being accepted and adored for my quirky differences.

However, my struggles with my sexuality are never far from my mind and I am desperate to subdue these inner demons.

TIM AND ROD SATTLER-JONES

When I discover I have an endless supply of booze and drugs at my disposal, I jump headfirst into the deep end.

The shame and self-hatred I feel don't go away, but now I have something far more effective to block it out than *The Simpsons*, coffee and Facebook. Alcohol fills the void of uncertainty inside me. When I'm drunk, I'm not questioning my every action, I'm not lost in my own depressive thoughts and I'm not scared and anxious about what my life will look like if I am Gay. I even feel like I'm rebelling against society's non-acceptance of me. The more I drink, the better I feel. And if the booze makes me feel this good, then surely drugs will make me feel even better, right? Lots of people smoke pot in Canada and I feel like I'd be a fool not to try it.

I first smoke marijuana with a girl I'm trying to impress (okay, lose my virginity to – that's why I'm here, after all). She works at the hotel with me and is a Canadian Miley Cyrus look-alike. I'm obsessed with Miley Cyrus and it occurs to me that I might be gravitating towards her doppelgänger out of the sheer desire not to be with her but to *be* her. This Miley look-alike loves smoking marijuana, hitting the wacky tobacky multiple times a day. I decide that to impress her I need to make out I'm really interested in smoking weed.

One day we're sitting alone together in a snow-covered secret garden in the hotel grounds. Miley is of course smoking a big joint and I summon my courage.

'Can I have a puff?'

Miley passes over the joint, and after puffing away multiple times I declare, 'Nothing's happening, I feel exactly the same as before.'

Then it hits me.

A huge wave of anxiety washes over me and I immediately start to panic. My heart is beating ridiculously fast and I keep thinking I'm going to swallow my tongue and die. *I am going to die. Right here in Canada. After my first puff on a joint.* This is the most intense anxiety and fear I have ever experienced in my life and it just goes on forever.

Miley is absolutely horrified at what is happening before her eyes and I can tell she feels extremely sorry for me. In an attempt to make me feel better, she offers to take me back to her room, where she can try to calm me down in privacy.

She gets me some water and we sit together on her bed listening to relaxing music. After an hour, I slowly start to feel a little better. Until, that is, Miley decides to stand up, rip her top off and hastily remove her bra.

She climbs on my lap and straddles me, and suddenly I'm staring straight at her large breasts. The marijuana gave me an anxiety attack but it has obviously had the opposite effect on Miley, making her horny. She leans forward, pressing her boobs directly into my face. Gasping for air, I begin to motorboat Miley's boobs and lick her nipples. I cannot help but wish it was Luke sitting on top of me with his big juicy pecs in my face. Miley grabs my hands and places them on her ass while she passionately kisses me. Then she pulls back and stares at me with seduction in her eyes.

I snap back to reality and I know the only way I can save myself is to follow Miley's lead and have sex with her. I'm determined to not only have sex with her and lose my virginity but also give her the greatest sex of her life so she forgets the pathetic marijuana meltdown she just witnessed.

I'm incredibly nervous but know this will help me prove to the world I'm straight. Miley slowly leans back in and starts kissing me again. I know from porn that following this we'll start foreplay and give each other head, which terrifies me even more. As she undoes my pants and begins to give me a blow job, I picture Luke in my head. No matter how much I try, I cannot stop wishing that Miley were a man. I act like I'm enjoying every second of her sexual attentions – and now it's my turn to return the favour.

As I slowly make my way down her body, kissing her as I go, my heart starts racing; I've never seen a vagina up close in real life, let alone licked one. As I come face to face with Miley's, I can't help being horrified. *What the fuck is that?* I'm disgusted by what is no doubt a nice vagina, if you like that sort of thing, and struggle to keep my erection. I quickly get Miley into the missionary position and rip open a condom.

This is it: the moment I go from boy to man, the moment I've longed for. Goodbye, virginity! I grab my dick to put on the condom that I've had saved in my wallet for the past few months. My heart sinks. I've totally lost my erection!

We're kissing the whole time, on her single bed with the lights dimmed. No matter how much I try to get turned on by this beautiful woman in front of me I'm wishing I could open my eyes and my roommate Luke would be looking up at me with a seductive grin on his face. I feel like a kid in a candy store who is allergic to candy. I feel totally embarrassed and ashamed of myself.

'What's wrong?' Miley asks.

'Um, I think I have whisky dick,' I mutter and roll over.

'What? You're kidding.' Miley's puzzled, then as I get up and grab my clothes I can tell she's angry – she's obviously very horny and my limp penis definitely isn't going to get her off. When I leave I'm at an all-time low – not only was I not able to have sex with a woman, I couldn't stop thinking of a man during the whole ordeal.

The following day I jump online to google a way to fix my 'gayness' and make it possible for me to have sex with Miley. I search for what seems like hours but finally come across a local chemist that sells sexual enhancement tablets. I feel so embarrassed just thinking about purchasing the tablets, but that's nothing compared to the embarrassment I felt last night.

I build up the courage and catch the bus down to the chemist to buy the magic sex pills. I'm wearing sunglasses and a big, hooded jacket trying to go undercover. I'm in and out as quickly as possible and for the entire way home I keep praying that the tablets will fix my erection and allow me to officially lose my virginity.

I text Miley and ask if I can come to her room. When she says yes, I take double the recommended dosage and head to Miley's room feeling like I'm walking on death row.

Miley opens the door. Before I can even offer her a fake seductive smile, she blurts out, 'We can't have sex, it's that time of the month.' Sheer joy radiates through my entire body.

Thank god, we don't have to have sex! While I'm not completely certain Miley actually has her period, she's just saved us both the embarrassment of facing the truth that I'm gay.

Although now, what am I going to do with this massive erection that won't go away? Over the next couple of hours I masturbate over gay porn about five times until my raging erection subsides. Maybe six. I guess I shouldn't have double dosed.

I decide to go out and drink my fear, anxiety and sorrows away. I gather a group of my friends and we head to the biggest nightclub in town. The club is a filthy hot mess. It stinks like balls, the floor is sticky and the bartenders are notoriously rude but for some reason it is always the best place in town to party the night away. A thick layer of smoke fills the club, and the place feels full beyond capacity with thirsty young travellers drinking themselves into intoxicated zombies.

Tonight I'm not messing around: I need to get the drunkest I have ever been. I need to be able to silence the voice that keeps yelling at me, *DUDE YOU'RE GAY!*

The club is packed to the rafters. There's laser lights everywhere, and LMFAO's song 'Shots' blasting on repeat. The dance floor is raging, everyone's groping each other and sticking their tongues down some random stranger's throat.

As I knock back shot after shot, my worries about being gay start to fade away. But that's not enough. I need to eliminate the failed sex attempt from my memory completely. I keep drinking until I can't see straight. The hundreds of flashing neon lights are beginning to merge into one huge dancing rainbow of music and smoke.

I take one more shot. Then everything goes black.

When I open my eyes I'm lying on a cold concrete floor and there are bright lights shining down on me. I sit up, frantically trying to figure out where I am. *Where the hell am I?* I look to my left. Two other men are lying lifeless on the floor and there's an old rusty toilet bowl in the corner filling the room with a disgusting stench. To my right there's a huge, reinforced, indestructible-looking barred door. The walls are dark grey and there's no natural light. It feels like an underground army bunker, or that scene in the *Saw* movies where everyone's held captive and tortured.

I've been kidnapped and am being held hostage. I push my head up against the metal bars of the door and with my heart in my chest yell, 'Hello!'

I hear footsteps coming. My heart starts beating even quicker now. *Is this the person who will torture us all? Am I going to be murdered or left for dead in a pool of blood?*

As the footsteps get closer, I make out the figure walking towards me ...

It's a police officer, and he looks furious. He has a gun hanging from one side of his belt and a thick black baton hanging from the other. As I sit on the floor, he stands above me, his eyes scalding me through the bars that separate us.

'Where am I?' I ask.

He replies, 'You're in gaol. We found you last night so drunk you weren't able to walk, so we handcuffed you, put you in a police car, drove you here and locked you up.'

I can't believe it. I'm in prison, completely humiliated, but more so terrified and ashamed that I have been this stupid.

I have plenty of time to contemplate this as the hours tick by slowly. The officer refuses to tell me when I will be released. I fall asleep on the freezing concrete floor until a voice above me says, 'It's time to go. But first you'll need to have your mug shot taken.'

Once again, my heart sinks. As I'm escorted to another room, I see a camera propped up against a blank wall. The police officer hands me a black sign to hold with my name, the date and a lot of random numbers on it, just like you see in the movies. I stand there holding the sign while the blinding camera flash goes off in my face, so ashamed of myself. I feel like a total failure and, while the camera continues to flash, tears build up. I burst out crying, and then I'm escorted from the building by the police officer. As he opens the door to freedom and gestures with his hand for me to exit, he says sternly, 'This is the town's drunk tank. If you find yourself here again, you won't be let off so lightly.'

Terrified, I look up at him and sincerely say, 'I promise this will never happen again.'

I walk in the freezing cold to Banff Avenue, the city's main street, where I can catch a bus back up the mountain to the hotel. My clothes are covered in every alcohol under the sun, my hair's a mess and I'm sure those are chunks of vomit on my pants. Catching sight of myself in a window, I look like I just crawled out of a rat-infested dumpster.

My head's spinning but I'm somehow still able to reflect on this huge slap of reality. Sure, drinking helps me forget all my shame and insecurities about being gay, but I've gone too far. *This can't happen again*. I need to find the strength within to overcome my fear of the gay unknown.

Sadly, however, even as I tell myself these things on the walk of shame back home and pass the nightclub where it all took place last night, I'm planning the next drunken night out. Drinking is the best way I know to escape my reality and I am definitely not in a place where I'm willing to give it up. It's my lifeline to normality and not even being locked up in the drunk tank is going to change that.

The highlight of my whole trip to Canada is the Calgary Stampede, a ten-day event billed as the Greatest Outdoor Show on Earth. The entire city of Calgary shuts down for this event, which attracts over one million visitors each year and features one of the world's largest rodeos, a huge parade, stage shows, concerts and Chuckwagon Racing (where drivers in old-fashioned wagons led by thoroughbred horses race around a track). The huge showgrounds are filled with adrenaline rides, live music and markets as far as the eye can see. Shopfronts and buildings are all painted and decorated in cowboy themes with everyone wearing western cowboy wear.

In the weeks leading up to the stampede, a big group of us at the hotel save up money so we can go to Calgary, and hire a minibus to take us just over an hour's drive east of Banff.

Walking into the stampede is like entering my *Brokeback Mountain* fantasy but on steroids: thousands of men dressed up in cowboy gear and ready to party. This is like one of my wet dreams, and I can't believe what I'm seeing. But as mesmerised as I am by all the sexy cowboys, I make a conscious effort to remark only on how sexy the girls look done up in their western attire.

From the second we walk through the huge iron gates we spend all our time going from beer garden to beer garden drinking as much booze as possible. I'm living my ultimate gap-year fantasy: having all the freedom in the world to be as crazy and badly behaved as I can possibly imagine, surrounded by thousands of sexy cowboys wearing chaps and oversized cowboy hats and carrying whips. There's a very dominant masculine cowboy vibe throughout, which is a turn-on. But it's also intimidating, as I don't want to be caught checking out how nice all the cowboys' butts look in their tight jeans. I need to fit in, not stand out.

Mandy, Luke, me and the rest of our hotel crew completely throw ourselves right into the rodeo experience, fuelled by ridiculous amounts of beer.

During the spectacular fireworks finale there is a moment where I look around and everyone's kissing. Deep down I desperately wish I were standing hand in hand with my dream cowboy, locking lips with him as the fireworks burst into a million bright lights over our heads. But there's no way in hell this is ever going to happen.

I let out a hopeless sigh and make my way to the closest beer garden.

7

ROD: 'I'm seeing someone but it's not a girl'

The liberation I feel after finally telling my parents who I am (well, *part* of who I am) is short-lived. Almost immediately after I reveal myself as bisexual, Mum and Dad start talking about 'treatment'.

'Surely you need significant help,' says Mum.

'You're clearly sick if you think you like boys,' says Dad.

This is precisely what I have been so afraid of. All my fears are being realised. To hear these words come out of my parents' mouths destroys me: I feel like such a disgrace and a disappointment. I lock myself in my room and cry for hours as the scale of the situation begins to dawn on me. *Are they going to press charges? Will Dean get in trouble? Am I out now? Have I been abused? What will happen?* I know in my heart of hearts that I haven't been abused. Although I've been so confused about how I feel, I knew exactly what I was doing and I enjoyed it. Despite the shame I feel, I know this is right for me.

At no point did I ever think that my parents' first reaction would be to make an appointment with a psychologist to fix me. This blindsided me and completely stumped me. *Do Mum and Dad actually think there's something wrong with me, that I'm sick?* This is all I can think about.

I huddle in my room, in a panic, trying to think of an escape plan. *How can I get out of this?* Life is going to suck living under my parents' roof. All I want to do is call Dean and ask him to run away with me because he is the only one who can understand how I'm feeling. If Dean and I were to move to another city, another state or indeed another country, no one will know us, and we can be free to be ourselves. None of our family members or friends needs to know and we can forget all this pain. I have been so distant with Dean; will he even know what has just gone down? Will he be angry with me too? Will he even want to run away with me?

The only thing I know for sure is that my life has changed forever.

I don't want to leave my room. When I do eventually come out to eat, Mum and Dad tell me that they want me to get some help and speak to a psychologist. They are stuck on the concept that I have been sexually abused by an older man. I just stand there taking in what they are telling me. I can feel anger bubbling to the surface.

I have always kept my emotions in check when it comes to this secret but now I feel like I'm ready to explode. 'I don't need help!' I scream at them. 'There's nothing wrong with me, there's something wrong with both of you for doing this to me! Why can't you accept me for me?'

No matter how hard I try, no matter how loud I scream, no matter what insult I throw at them, they don't budge.

'I hate you!' I yell, storm down the hallway and slam my bedroom door.

Minutes later Dad opens the door and comes in. I glare at him like he is my worst nightmare, my rage rampant.

'Mate, I'm not here to fight with you,' he says, trying to speak calmly, 'but you need to get your head right and speak to someone about this. That mongrel took advantage of you and you need to speak to a professional about it.'

I finally explode. I stand up, push Dad into my wardrobe doors and scream, 'I have not been fucking abused! And there is nothing wrong with me!'

Dad is taken aback, then he gets mad. 'Don't you dare lay your hands on —'

'Get out of my room!' I cut him off.

Dad storms out and I slam the door behind him. I throw myself down on my bed, bury my face in my pillow and just cry and cry and cry.

I cannot help but think that my parents would prefer that I've been abused than for their son to be Gay. I can understand that my parents might think I'm fucked in the head if I'd actually been raped or abused but I haven't – and no matter how hard I try to convince them, they're not listening.

Without any further conversation, my parents make an appointment for a few days' time with a Christian psychologist, a woman who goes to my church. I've seen her around but never met her before. I've always been a little bit scared of her, to be honest, because I felt like she had the air of a mean school principal about her.

I don't want to speak to anyone about this, let alone a psychologist, and I certainly don't want to be 'fixed'. I've tried everything and I cannot be fixed.

I feel like I'm about to be admitted to a psych ward against my will. I put up a fight with my parents, desperately arguing my case. Nothing will budge them.

I'm hyperventilating while trying my hardest to explain that this isn't something new, that I've been battling this and praying to be healed for years. All my dad can say is, 'It's just not right mate, it's just not right.'

'Fight harder,' Mum says. 'Keep fighting. Don't let the devil win, Rod, he's beating you.'

We fight about it for hours. They have no idea the torture I go through and have been going through for years and years. I try to go down the bisexual path again and play down the gay side. I tell them, 'I still like girls and prefer girls. I just can't help that I'm attracted to boys too. I still want a wife and kids.' I'm scrambling and I can hear that what I'm saying makes no sense.

I eventually give in and scream at them, 'I'll go to the psychologist if you'll leave me alone!'

The day of the appointment arrives. Dad's going to drive me; there's no way he's going to let me drive myself because he knows I won't go.

I find the strength to fight one last time. 'Dad, I don't want to go to a bloody psychologist!'

'Rod, this is not up for discussion. Get in the car,' he says.

It's the most silent car ride I've ever endured. I just stare out the window like a prisoner being driven to gaol. I'm beyond nervous, petrified of what I'm about to walk into. I mean, I've never been to a psychologist before, let alone to discuss something so personal. I look over at Dad. His face is set in an angry expression but his eyes are watering, as though he's holding back tears and won't allow himself to cry in front of me. I think, *I have let Dad down like never before.*

The psychologist's office is in an old house that's been converted into medical suites. We go up a steep, tree-lined driveway to the front door. The closer we get, the more I want to throw up. Inside it's odd: there are chairs set up like a waiting room in what clearly used to be a lounge room and what looks like a reception area but there's no one behind the desk. A note on the desk reads 'Take a seat and someone will be with you shortly'. Dad and I sit on opposite sides of the room, in the same space but worlds apart. A few minutes pass and the psychologist walks in. I immediately remember that last time I responded in church and got prayed for out the front of the congregation, she was next to me. Today she has an extremely calm demeanour, very different from when I see her at church. Maybe it's just the copious amount of scented candles and the relaxing music.

'Hi Rod, how are you?' she asks, making a point of addressing me and not my dad. I wonder whether Mum and Dad have already given her the back story. She can probably tell just by looking at me that I'd rather be anywhere else in the world right now.

She shows me to her room while Dad stays in the waiting room – so I don't do a runner, I guess. The walls are filled with positive quotes and there's a lounge under a small window, a large armchair and the smell of yet more scented candles. In the middle there's a coffee table with only a notepad in a binder, a pen and her glasses on it.

The psychologist asks me to sit. Uncomfortable as all hell, I sink into the chair with my arms crossed, looking around the room for a clock. She takes the lounge.

We begin.

'What brings you here?'

I say nothing. I don't even know where to start.

'What do you want to talk about?' she tries again. 'Is there something you want to get off your chest?'

The psychologist keeps firing questions at me as I sit there in silence until finally I blurt out, 'My dad forced me to be here, I don't want to be here. I can't be fixed, so leave me alone.'

The psychologist doesn't react to my rudeness, as though this is the norm for her. I'm trying my best not to make eye contact with her and my anxiety is going through the roof.

'Let's just talk about how you're feeling now. Don't worry about why you're here or who made you come, just tell me how you are feeling right now.'

How I am feeling? *I want to jump out of that window and run for my life*, I think. But I wipe the tears from my eyes, look over at her and in frustration I start throwing words at her.

'I feel angry. I feel scared. I feel stupid. I am sooo confused. I just feel sick, I could literally vomit,' I tell her.

She jumps on this. 'Angry? What do you feel angry about, why are you angry?' And just like that I start opening up, though still being defensive, and explain to her that no one understands me or gets what I'm going through.

The psychologist goes through each word and gets me to explain why I'm feeling each emotion while she writes notes, which really creeps me out. *What is she writing about me?*

The hour feels like a lifetime. By the end of it I've opened up more than I thought I would, but still haven't told her the extent of what has just gone down. Wrapping up the session she looks at me and says, 'If you don't want to be here then don't come. You have to make the next appointment, not your dad, and you need to want to get help.'

This is all just too much. I can't handle it.

I can't stop the thoughts flooding my mind, and I know that Mum and Dad will make me come back anyway, so I make the next appointment.

I decide the only way forward is to accept my parents' version of events and go back into the closet. Living 'out' as a gay man is simply too hard and I can't ever put myself through this again.

My parents ask me all the time how my sessions are going and I keep telling them, 'They're going great, it's really helping gain control over my thoughts.'

Week after week I sit in the psychologist's office, giving a little bit more each time. I explain to her that I've done sexual things with a guy in his mid-twenties but that it wasn't abuse and I knew what I was doing. I tell her I've been attracted to guys since I was a child. I know I have to stick this out for a while to be convincing and, anyway, Dad's paying for it all. I have a plan: I will use the psychologist appointments to convince everyone I was confused, that I am in fact straight and that I've been 'fixed'.

I've been seeing the psychologist for three months when one day she says something that sticks with me:

'Think of your thoughts like a bus stop. You are waiting for the bus. A bus pulls up at the stop. You have a decision: do you get on that bus and ride it or wait for the next one? This is just like your thoughts. When a thought comes in like "I am gay", you have a choice. You can either accept that thought and hop on that bus or you can say no I am not going to believe that thought and I'll wait for the next bus.'

This is it. This is the analogy that I can use to convince my family I'm straight. Not that they're desperate to be convinced anymore; my plan has worked.

I tell Mum and Dad, 'I think this is what's been happening.

I'm believing these negative thoughts and I need to choose to wait for the next bus.' This is music to Mum's ears. I tell her that I want to focus back on church and my relationship with God again as I feel I've turned away from him a lot recently.

One day the psychologist says I don't need to continue with our sessions. I'm attending church regularly and my secret is safe once again. For all intents and purposes, I'm a happy straight Christian man. I feel so lucky I didn't tell more people.

I'm back at church, doing the same routine. Friday night, Youth Group; Saturday night, coffee with church crew; Sunday, church service followed by dinner with the church crew again. There's a beautiful girl in the group, Erin, who I'm growing really close to. I try to convince myself that this could be something; maybe I am bisexual after all or maybe I'll be able to fall for her. There are definitely feelings here, but to what extent? I'm not sure.

Erin is a few years older than me; she is gorgeous and has a great heart. But nothing inside me wants to rip her clothes off like I wanted to do with Dean or my old high school teacher. It's just not the same as it is with guys. We hang out a lot and it doesn't take long for her to become my official girlfriend, with a little encouragement from both our mums. In my mind she is the perfect Christian girl, she ticks all my parents' boxes and I genuinely enjoy spending time with her. *We could get married and have a family together*, I think, but that perfect picture wouldn't be fair to me or to her, would it? We've been dating for a few months and every night I'm still masturbating to gay porn in my bedroom. I feel guilty about it, like in a weird way I'm cheating on her.

One afternoon Mum pulls me aside for yet another talk. *I've been hiding everything so well so why am I getting another talking to?* We sit down on the lounge and Mum pulls out a ring. It's her original engagement ring, the one Dad gave her when he proposed. (Mum upgraded years ago.) It's so shiny and gold, with this big diamond on it.

'I want you to give this to your girlfriend,' Mum says.

'I'm not proposing, Mum. I'm only seventeen,' I quickly reply.

She explains to me that it's not an engagement ring but a promise ring to give to Erin until I'm financially secure enough to propose and for us to get married. Mum tells me she has already been in touch with my Erin's mum to find out her ring size and has already had the ring sized to fit her finger.

In an effort to keep up this facade, I accept the ring, thank her for the gesture and start to plan a date when I can give it to Erin.

Our date is like something out of a 1950s movie. We drive to this beautiful spot on the top of a cliff overlooking the beach. I've packed some food and soft drinks and set the mood perfectly. (Mum has always told me that I'm a romantic and someday I'll make a girl incredibly happy.) The sun goes down and we look out over the ocean, which has turned stunning shades of pink and orange.

I decide the time is right and pull out Mum's ring. I can't read Erin's face; I'm not sure if she's excited because she thinks I'm about to propose or whether she's about to shut me down as we've only been together such a short time. I quickly say, 'This isn't an engagement ring.' I tell her that I have strong feelings for her and that I want her to wear this ring as a 'promise ring' until we're able to get engaged.

She claps her hands excitedly, keeps looking at the ring and saying over and over, 'You're so cute.' She is always talking about marriage and kids and I think she is expecting more, like she is waiting for me to say 'I love you' but I just can't – so I don't. She accepts the ring and I don't even get a kiss. *Are you for real?* We've been together for months and the most action I get is some hand-holding, a hug and an occasional peck on the cheek. I'm not expecting sex, but a kiss isn't that much to ask for and, in this moment, I can't help but think back to what I had with Dean. I try to convince myself that if I can have some form of physical connection with a girl then this will prove to me that I'm able to make a life with a girl and may even like it. Dean loved to kiss me and make me feel amazing sexually and my girlfriend won't even give me a little kiss in this romantic setting. I needed this to see how it made me feel. And I just don't even know if deep down I feel disappointed about it.

The entire relationship just feels fake to me and I know no matter how hard I try I'm probably going to end up hurting Erin, who has done nothing wrong. My family and I have been hiding my secret past and I'm never planning on telling my girlfriend any of it. We don't have a physical relationship; I don't know if I can have with her what I had with Dean, and meanwhile, despite my romantic gestures, she won't kiss me. Is this because she suspects something or is she picking up a vibe? Has she heard something on the rumour mill? Or is that we just have zero chemistry?

One day just before my eighteenth birthday, Erin texts me to come over to 'talk'. *Oh shit, she knows.* I ask her if everything is okay and she replies, 'Yep, just want to talk.' I jump in my car and drive over to her place.

Her mum answers the door with a sad look on her face. She says to me, 'Hi Rod, Erin's in her room, come on in.' *Who died?* I think. The energy in the house is terrible. *What am I walking into?*

I go into Erin's room, leaving the door open as per the rules of the house – we couldn't be alone with the door shut. She's sitting on the bed and I stand at the end, anxiously waiting for what she has to say. She has this awkward smile on her face and can hardly make eye contact with me. She fidgets with a pillow. 'Rod, I'm just going to jump right on in because this is really hard,' she says.

Okay …

'I … I don't think our paths align with the will of God. We can't be together anymore. I know this is right, so please understand.' As she is speaking she pulls Mum's ring off her hand and gives it back to me. I take it, walk out the house and back to my car. As I drive home, I don't know if what I'm feeling is relief or panic.

I pull up in the driveway and walk back inside. Mum's in the kitchen making herself a cup of tea.

She looks up and says, 'That was quick.'

I walk over to her and give her the ring and say, 'She dumped me.' Out of nowhere, I burst into tears. So many emotions hit me at once. I don't have a cover anymore; I can't hide who I am by talking about my girlfriend. I'm also upset out of a sense of failure. I tried to come out and failed, and I tried to settle down and live the life that was expected of me and failed. I feel so lost and down on myself. Mum tries to cheer me up and I just say, 'I'm so hurt, I thought she could be the one.'

Why do I keep lying?

Turning eighteen means that I'm an adult and can drink and party. I move out of Mum and Dad's house and into a unit with my cousin Faith. She's an open-minded and gorgeous soul but even so, I don't want to come clean with her.

I attend church less and party more, going out to clubs every weekend. I make it my mission every time I go out to pash on with some random girl on the dance floor. I make a lot of new friends who aren't Christian and I slowly distance myself from all my Christian circles where I feel judgement.

On Sundays I often still go to church, just hungover. Mum still goes to the traditional Baptist Church but I've moved churches to the one I used to go to when I was at youth group, so Mum really doesn't know how often I'm attending.

One day at church, I meet another girl, Lauren; she's not like any of the other girls I've met before and we become friends straightaway. She has hair like a mermaid and the most gorgeous blue eyes. I ask her to go for a walk down by the foreshore. She tells me about the two guys she's had sex with in the past but, not only that, she also casually tells me that her ex is a female.

Another person just like me! Well, in female form.

I tell Lauren that I'm technically still a virgin, but that I've fooled around with another guy. We stay out talking for hours. This is the first person that I can relate to since Dean, and it feels incredible. She tells me that she's bisexual and that it's okay to be different.

The following night I ask Lauren around to hang out. I cook her my famous spaghetti bolognese; Faith is out for the night and we have the unit to ourselves. We decide to go into the bedroom. I sense that she wants to kiss me. I lean in and give her a kiss as she slides her hand down the front of my pants. To my surprise, I'm really hard. Within moments we're both naked and she's giving me head. She rolls over onto her back and pulls me on top of her and tells me it's okay. I have no idea what I'm doing so she grabs my dick and guides me inside her. It doesn't take long for me to finish, which I feel bad about and, just like that, I've lost my virginity to a woman. And then we do it again.

We had a great time but this just fucks with my head even more. I want men, I fantasise about men, I look at gay porn – but I was just able to get hard and have sex with a woman.

A few days later I tell Lauren I don't want anything further. I feel like a bastard, but I need to be honest with myself. I would have much preferred her to have been a man.

I spend the next year or two partying up a storm and trying to distance myself from the church as much as possible. When I'm twenty, I decide to go to Europe on a Contiki tour. Just me, on an adventure of a lifetime, with twenty-five other young people ready to party.

On my flight over, I battle with my thoughts again. Do I come clean to my Contiki group and try to hook up with guys, or keep playing the straight card and just see if I can get hard again?

When I arrive I notice there's only a handful of guys on tour and the rest are gorgeous girls. I get a lot of attention from the girls and quickly decide there is no way I am telling them my secret.

Night one, in Croatia, we have a pirate-themed party. One of the girls is throwing herself at me and we're all wasted. She leads me to the roof where she proceeds to take her clothes off and then remove mine. This time I'm having a few issues getting hard. I tell her it's just the booze, and she spends the next ten minutes doing her best to get him up. I decide to close my eyes and fantasise that there's a fit man with me on the rooftop. Just like that, he rises to the occasion and we end up having sex.

Over the six-week trip, having sex with girls becomes an exercise in proving I'm straight or at least able to get hard with girls, even if I do need to fantasise about men most of the time. Every sexual partner is a notch on my 'I'm straight' belt. I'm actually miserable but if my family are happy and no one knows my secret then I'll keep ticking along. I just can't deal with any more disappointment from them and there's no way I want to see that look on their faces again.

At a chalet in the Swiss Alps, I get absolutely plastered. There are multiple other tour groups there and this massive club attached to the chalet. I drink so many tequila shots it's going down like water. I dance and make out with a blonde American bombshell called Emily from one of the other groups all night, and I'm pretty certain she's coming back to my room tonight. I need some air so I ask her to come outside with me. It's frosty up there in the mountains and as we lean up against one of the bus tyres she cuddles into me and starts asking me about my life. In my drunken state, I think it's a good idea to pour out my heart.

I start talking about work and my friends, then I start to talk about my family and suddenly tears start falling. I tell her that things are okay at the moment but will turn to shit when I tell them the truth.

She looks puzzled. 'The truth?' she asks.

I look her in the eye and say, 'I don't really want to have sex with you, I think I might be gay.' As I finish speaking my tears turn into sobbing.

The gorgeous, romantic full moon is shining down on the snow-capped mountains and here I am, a blubbering mess. Emily just stares at me in silence as I sit there crying. Not surprisingly, she doesn't want to have sex with me anymore.

In many ways, this trip is incredible. I get my nipple pierced in London, my ear pierced in Paris, I parasail in Austria, party in all the best nightclubs across Europe, visit the leaning tower of Pisa and even eat spaghetti bolognese in the town of Bologna where it originated (the Aussie version is better). But it doesn't resolve anything. I've slept with so many beautiful, amazing girls, unburdened myself to strangers and lived outside of my Christian bubble for a while – not to mention seeing the world!

When I get back home to Newcastle, though, I'm the same old me, with the same old feelings and secrets. Partying is the only relief available to me so I continue going out as much as possible and try to take each day at a time. I just don't know what else to do.

Not long after I return from my trip, I score a new job as a teller with a local bank. On the first day of training, I meet a guy called Jeremy (Jez). He's very confident and a bit over the top but I love it. Jez lives close to me so we decide to carpool together for the rest of the two-week training at head office. We pump tunes in the car and dance up a storm. I think Jeremy is giving off some vibes but he keeps talking about his girlfriend so I'm a bit confused.

Everyone in training gets assigned the branch they will work out of so the carpooling stops until a couple of months later at the next training day. This time on the drive Jez tells me that he and his girlfriend have broken up and then, subtly yet not-so-subtly, starts asking if I know any gay people. I am so confused about why he's asking me this. *Am I giving him vibes?* He tells me he knows these twin brothers and one of them is gay. I don't know where my confidence comes from but I say, 'Are you into guys?'

'Are you?' Jez fires back.

'I asked you first.'

'Well yeah, I think I am bi.'

'OMG, I am into dudes too but no one knows,' I say, then we both let out high-pitched screams. We talk about it the rest of the way to work, on the way home from work and then it consumes every conversation. It's our secret that we're just not ready to tell anyone else.

For my 21st birthday, my friends and I have arranged a party to go to Future Music Festival in Sydney. We book a bus and everything. On board are my closest friends, including my best mate, Mitch. We've been friends since school and have become even closer since. He's my rock, and great fun to party with. But as close as we are, I'm afraid of losing this friendship because of my sexual preference so I've decided to keep it to myself for now.

Also on board the bus are Jez and a bunch of his friends, people I've never met, including these twin brothers, one of whom keeps smiling at me the way Dean used to. *Could he be like me?* I wonder. Then it clicks. *This is the gay twin Jez had told me about.*

Halfway to Sydney, we're all smashed. Shots, goon bags, you name it, we're drinking it. Everyone keeps making me skol because it's my birthday. Drunk me is not so good at hiding my true self and I get a little loud and my inner gay boy tries to make an appearance. I can't stop wondering whether this dude who keeps smirking at me is like me. I get up and decide to go introduce myself. His name is Adam. We have a shot together and make small talk.

I start to get a bit flirty. Subtle enough that no one knows but open enough to show my intentions. I begin with an 'accidental' graze of his side ass and a hand on his leg, and it doesn't take long before Adam is reciprocating. We exchange phone numbers and I head back to my seat before anyone can get suss. There's thousands of people at the festival and we're all off our heads on party drugs and alcohol so Adam and I lose each other.

Back home, after I recover from my crazy hangover, I decide to shoot Adam a message to see if he wants to hang out. He's keen and we arrange to meet by the lake, the same spot I went with Dean a few years back. We go for a walk and this time I don't hesitate to ask him if he's into boys. I have no idea where this confidence is coming from.

He tells me he's been with a couple of guys and that he's gay, and he pleads with me to not tell anyone. Déjà vu! Dean had said almost those exact same words. I come clean straightaway and tell Adam that I'm into guys but I've never had sex with one. Just like with Dean, I feel a spark and sexual tension between us.

We head back to the car, go for a drive to a secluded location and fool around. I'm really nervous, and my heart starts racing. I've never let myself go all the way with a guy because I've always felt like that would be very final ... but now I'm here, and I want to do it so bad. I tell Adam that I'm not ready for him to do me, and he says he's happy to take that role. We move to the back seat.

There are no other cars in sight, but while I'm so worried about being caught in the act, I'm too horny to stop now.

There's hardly any room so we move the front seats as far forward as they'll go. Adam removes his shirt and pants and then starts pulling my pants off too. He straddles me and begins to kiss me. He certainly seems to know what he's doing, which I'm glad of because I have no idea really.

'Do you want to get in me?' Adam whispers as he reaches for the bottle of lube on the seat next to us.

This is it. I just nod.

Adam squirts some lube into his hand, reaches behind himself to put some on his ass and then grabs a condom. He unrolls it on my dick and starts to stroke me. I feel like I could come just from that. He then sits back and ever so slowly guides my dick inside him, moving up and down until I'm all the way in.

This feels incredible. In a strange way I feel so liberated, like this is right and what I'm supposed to be doing. We stay in that position because we don't have space, but it's also super hot to be able to kiss Adam while thrusting inside him.

It's not long until I'm ready to blow. 'I'm about to come,' I say and he says, 'Me too.' We come just seconds apart and it's the most intense orgasm I've ever had.

I thought I'd be riddled with guilt afterwards but I just want to do it all over again – and after seeing how much Adam enjoyed it, I'm curious to know if I'll like being on the receiving end.

Before long we become official boyfriends – well, officially to each other. We spend a lot of quality time together, though I wish I could see more of him. He always seems to have family dinners on or drinks with his cousins, which of course I don't want to intrude on, and he comes over afterwards anyway. He tells me he was seeing someone before me but it's over now – sometimes they still text him. I get the impression they're not quite over him, but he assures me it's all in the past.

We keep our relationship a secret for a while, and to all our friends and family we're just friends who met at a music festival. Eventually we decide to come out to all our closest friends.

I decide to come out to Mitch. My best friend since Year 7, I love him like a brother. I'm so nervous about telling him because I'm afraid it'll damage the relationship we have. I drive down to his house, in a beautiful spot right on the lake. We go for a walk to the takeaway shop, get our favourite special wedges, smothered in sour cream, sweet chilli sauce and cheese, and go over the road to sit by the lake.

Looking out over the water, I think, *This is going to be so awkward.* I gather up my courage and then just blurt it out: 'I'm seeing someone, a guy.'

I expected a silence or weirdness but all Mitch does is shrug his shoulders and reply, 'Oh cool, who is he?' He doesn't seem to have a care in the world. 'You're my family,' he says. 'I love you unconditionally and I want you to be happy.'

I am stunned by this reaction, but Mitch goes on, 'You can't help who you fall for Rod, there's nothing wrong with this.'

Suddenly I feel normal. After feeling for so long like I have a sickness or a disease, this is amazing. It's as though the huge weight I placed on my shoulders when I tried to be straight has lifted.

I'm now old enough and confident enough to finally live the life I want. I just cannot keep hiding anymore.

It feels almost inevitable at this point: I need to tell my parents. I know this won't go down well and my brain flashes back to when I was seventeen years old and the whole thing with Dean. I don't have the capacity to endure that pain again but I convince myself that surely, after all these years, they'll understand it's not a phase and that I am indeed gay. Surely it can't be as bad as the first time. At least this time I don't live under their roof.

I drive over to my parents' place, my heart almost beating out of my chest. As I get out of the car, my parents look out the window, thrilled to see me. To them it would seem like a normal day, a normal visit – but I know I'm carrying a grenade into the house.

There are hellos, kisses and cuddles at the door but I'm a man on a mission. I have to tell them.

'I need to talk to you,' I say.

I can see on their faces that they know something's wrong. As they sit down in the lounge room, my sister Emma lingers in the corner.

'Mum, Dad, I'm seeing someone,' I say.

'Yeah?' Dad says, looking at Mum with a confused look on his face.

'But it's not a girl.'

Mum and Dad both tear up. Dad can't even look at me, which hurts more than anything he could say … but the words hurt too.

All bloody hell breaks loose.

'This is wrong,' they say.

'So, by seeing someone, you mean you're having sex with a man?'

'Do you actually enjoy a penis in your bum? That's disgusting.'

I break down in tears but this time all I feel is rage. Shame and upset is now replaced by fire.

Years of anger roll out as I scream, *I can't be fixed! I was born this way. Why can't you just love me for me?'*

I can't get through to them no matter what I say. Through gritted teeth, I say to them, 'You are dead to me. If you can't accept me then you no longer exist. I no longer have parents.'

I storm out of the house, believing it's likely the last time I'll ever see them.

I can't believe this is happening again. I have to do what's best for me and my own happiness. I'm choosing my true self over a relationship with my family.

But have I made the right decision?

8

TIM: My inner critic is a piece of shit!

It's a typical sunny Newcastle afternoon. The air's thick with humidity and over the drone of lawnmowers and lazy traffic you can hear a ref's whistle and the roar of a crowd from the nearby footy oval.

Untypically, I'm standing in the backyard with the hot sun beating down on me, about to do a boxing and ab workout with my eldest brother, Ben. I'm cautious as I know I'm very unfit after my time away in Canada, but I want to be proactive about trying to get my health back.

As we begin the workout, I'm already covered in sweat from the heat. My brother rips his shirt off and carries on in just his shorts. I feel self-conscious of my body and pasty skin but it's a scorcher so I rip my shirt off too. Maybe I can get a bit of a tan. I can't help but admire and also feel envious of how my brother looks. He is super fit, lean and tanned. 'I really want to get in shape so I can look like you,' I pant in one of the few rests breaks I'm allowed. Ben is my idol and embodies everything I want to be: strong, fast, fit, lean and most of all popular!

It's soul-destroying to be failing so miserably at all the physical challenges he's setting for me. Everything I try to do he not only does ten times faster but also isn't keeling over in pain by the end of it or about to shit himself and projectile vomit like I am. The grass has been freshly cut so after multiple rounds of army crawls on the ground we're both covered from head to toe in grass clippings. Ben looks like the Incredible Hulk, and I look like Dipsy the green Teletubby.

My relationship with Ben is okay. We don't have anything in common, but he's definitely done his best to help me when I need it. I want to be like him so bad and he's been happy to show me how to do the things he's pretty much famous for around town – surfing, rugby and fitness. He tried to teach me how to surf multiple times, but it always ended with me being wiped out over and over. I'm also terrified of sharks so with the combination of repetitive wipe-outs and ridiculous non-existent shark sightings, I threw in the towel.

The next area in which I tried to emulate him was rugby league. After much deliberation I decided it would be a good idea, seeing as my brother is captain of the local rugby league team the Wanderers and basically famous at the rugby club, to enrol myself in a lower age grade and give it a shot. I showed up to the first training session not knowing anyone. The coach saw the name Sattler and his eyes lit up. He welcomed me to the team with open arms, thinking I was going to be their next superstar player.

In the forty-five-minute training session I proceeded to drop every single pass thrown my way, was constantly on the verge of tears from being tackled too hard and, the cherry on top, I stubbed my toe and squealed. I humiliated myself in front of the entire rugby team. Showing my face anywhere near those people or the rugby field ever again would be social suicide.

So I've ticked surfing and rugby league off my list of ways to be more like my brother. Now all that's left is fitness, which brings me back to our current workout.

My brother looks me up and down. 'You're going to need to do a lot more core exercises to get rid of this sloppiness here,' he says, grabbing my belly fat and poking at my rolls. I know he's joking but it still cuts deeply. It sounds so much like the humiliating comments I endured throughout school. Somehow, I hold myself together for the remainder of the workout, but even as my stomach muscles burn and my gloves pound the pads, I replay his remark. When we finish I quickly throw my shirt back on, feeling like a failure and a pathetic fat piece of shit. My self-confidence was already low but now it's completely non-existent.

I run inside and jump straight into the shower to wash the copious amounts of dirt, sweat and grass off. After my shower I stand naked in the bathroom, staring at myself in the mirror and feeling enraged, completely disgusted by what I see. I have huge gross man boobs, bulging love handles and fat thighs that feel like they're jiggling even while I'm standing still. My once-defined stomach has now turned to fat and my previously strong jawline is drowning in double chins. My face is covered in pimples and

I don't even want to turn around and look at my fat saggy ass cheeks. Months and months of relentless partying in Canada have taken their toll and left me in the most unfit shape of my life. I can't bear to look anymore and quickly wrap a towel around me.

The tears start to flow. *How could I have done this to myself?*

The transition from Canada to Australia is tough to say the least. Coming home is a massive wake-up call for me to start getting my shit together and following the road I want pursue. In Canada I could do whatever I wanted without any responsibility, party hard and burn through all my money. But now I feel immense pressure to go to uni, get a professional job and earn a lot of money. I already feel like such a complete failure compared to my brothers and friends. And I don't want to let Mum down. Her best friends' kids are studying law and architecture and becoming doctors and here I am – a fat, broke loser who wanted to be a famous back-up dancer.

I'm as confused as ever about who I am and what I want out of life, so the safest option seems to be to follow everyone else my age and go to uni and score a nine-to-five office job. This is my worst nightmare; I did dance and drama at a performing arts school for god's sake! But, as always, I ignore my true inner callings and take the safe road. As much as I want to entertain people, make them smile and forget about their worries, I definitely don't have the courage to break away from the crowd.

So I start a Bachelor of Business at the University of Newcastle. Not only is it not what I truly want, but I'm in poor shape for starting a new life chapter – physically, emotionally and mentally. I'm confused about my sexual identity, disgusted with my physical appearance and showing major signs of anxiety. I'm always nervous, and my hands seem to shake uncontrollably. My heart beats rapidly, I fumble over my words in conversation and I cannot maintain eye contact. This all weighs heavily on my heart, and it feels like a struggle to remain sane with all the hatred and anger raging inside me. There is only one thing that helps.

I've come home from Canada with a well-established reliance on alcohol and I use it to numb every part of my existence. When I'm happy I drink, when I'm sad I drink and whenever I'm nervous, excited, anxious, or mad I … you guessed it, DRINK! Alcohol helps me to avoid all my internal problems – and they're multiplying.

The negative hate-filled voice in my head will not let up and now it feels like my physical appearance exactly matches how I feel on the inside. Every day I stand in front of the bathroom mirror and catalogue my faults. I know deep down I'm gay but, looking like this, what gay man is going to want me? If I want to fit into the gay world, I cannot look like this. If I can't get control over my mind, then it's my mission to regain control over my body.

I decide I need to lose as much weight as I can and get as skinny as humanly possible. In front of the mirror I open my towel one last time and take a mental photo of my shameful naked body. *You will never be this fat, gross and disgusting ever again*, I declare.

Every day seems to be a never-ending mental and physical struggle. I keep trying to look on the bright side of life, but every single morning I wake up on the wrong side of the bed and can't seem to shake my inner anger and frustration. I feel like I've had the life sucked out of me. I know that I'm my own worst enemy because my life truly isn't that bad – I have a loving family, my own car and I'm still living rent-free at home. Still, it feels like I'm at war with myself and this ongoing self-hatred is resulting in depression and emptiness. Worse, there seems to be no end in sight.

For the past few years, my inner critic has been like a song on repeat, drilling negativity, self-doubt and hate into my head. By this point it feels like anything could push me to breaking point. I'm hanging on by a thread and if I can't find a way to stop this inner voice, I don't want to live anymore.

Despite my inner turmoil, I try my hardest to smile for the world. I've become a professional at the fake laugh and should probably win an Oscar for my fraudulent starring role in my own life. The winner of the most believable phony happiness award goes to … Tim Sattler.

But maybe my struggles are beginning to show to my close family and friends. I've shut everyone out of my life, after all. I would rather be trapped alone in my negative state of mind than have others see me at my lowest point, so I don't answer phone calls and use any excuse to steer clear of social interaction.

I decline invitations to attend friends' birthday parties, I cancel lunch and dinner plans with my family, I even concoct multiple excuses to cancel shifts at work.

My job on the reception desk of a local hotel is causing me stress. I'm often left on my own and the phone rings off the hook, guests frequently wanting things brought to their room and angry guests wanting to change rooms because it's not what they booked online. The hotel is trying to cut costs so most of the time there's only one person to juggle all of these tasks. On many shifts I shake uncontrollably and hide in the back office having panic attacks.

I decide to volunteer for the graveyard shifts because there's little guest interaction. The negative side of doing these shifts is coming home at 8 am when everyone else is heading out to work. I really struggle to get to sleep but soon realise that a few glasses of wine helps.

It's getting too hard to maintain my facade and I'm scared people will notice that I look anxious, and view my trembling hands and shaky voice as weakness.

I'm over faking that I'm okay. Everyone can just fuck off because I would rather be alone than forced to face the truth: I'm losing the battle with my inner demons.

Thankfully I'm getting one part of my life under control, and that's food intake and working out. I'm obsessed with fixing my physical appearance. Now every day my one and only goal is to eat as few calories as possible and do as much cardio exercise as I can. Exercising not only helps me burn the weight I so desperately want to lose, but it also offers me a fleeting moment of peace and quiet in my mind. Exercising has a similar effect to drinking – I don't feel ashamed, embarrassed or sad that I'm gay or scared about my future as a gay man living in this world. When I'm running, I feel empowered, invigorated and excited to be alive. But the second the exercise ends it's as if I'm sobering up and the negative feelings flood back in.

I figure it's not rocket science. The formula for a happy, anxiety-free life is: exercise frequently, restrict calories and get drunk as often as possible. If I follow this, I'll not only feel more in control of my body and mind, but it'll also help to stop my inner voice screaming pure hatred at me.

I exercise multiple times a day and have cut out all sugars, fats and carbohydrates. For breakfast, lunch and dinner I eat only the lowest calorie foods I can possibly find. I exercise for hours on end, to the point of exhaustion, and then eat only carrots, say. For a few weeks, I live on sugar-free drinks and celery, and it takes its toll. I'm dizzy, nauseous and always cold. I frequently get heart palpitations and painful stomach cramps, and I'm constantly lethargic.

I'm basically a walking zombie who won't even eat a brain because it has too many calories.

It's dinner time. *You need to eat*, I reluctantly tell myself. As I drag myself out of bed, my entire body begs for nutrients as it struggles to walk. I make my way down the hallway to the kitchen, stopping frequently so I don't fall over during the headspins.

In the kitchen I slowly open the fridge door. It's an effort. None of my family is at home so I have the privacy to concoct the lowest-calorie meal possible.

I look like skin and bone; it's plain for everyone to see. I've become very defensive and try to disguise my scrawny frame with the baggiest clothes I can find. It's common for people to come out with, 'You look anorexic,' or 'Are you eating enough?' This only motivates me further, and in a way I use my eating disorder to get revenge not only on myself but also on everyone in my life who, although they care for me, doesn't understand or accept me.

Now I'm always shivering and feel freezing, wherever I go. My stomach hurts all the time, and I'm having extreme mood swings. Deep down I know exactly why, but I don't care. Restricting food, over exercising and constantly drinking is my lifeline, and nothing on planet Earth is ever going to make me stop.

It's not just the reprieve from my inner critic that's so addictive – I also need to look like the gay men I see on the internet. I still haven't been with a man; however, I'm continually googling naked men. Every single gay man I see has ridiculously defined six-pack abs, massive biceps and zero body fat. I'm so desperate to be like them. I think if I look like these men on the internet I won't hate myself anymore.

The little I know about the gay community is that they're accepting in so many ways, but it's also a place of judgement, shame and unachievable body expectations. I know I'm gay and, as liberating as the thought of being myself is, I feel that if I want to eventually be a part of this community, I need to look like the chiselled Greek gods I see in gay porn.

I'm in a constant cycle of denial, anxiety and compulsive behaviour, spiralling deeper and deeper into a dark hole of addiction – and I have no desire to scream for help.

I scan the fridge. Steak. *Too much fat*. Leftover pasta. *Way too many carbohydrates*. Mum's famous chicken stir-fry. *Too much salt and sugar*.

The only thing catching my eye is a tub of yogurt lurking in the back of the fridge. The words 'No fat, no sugar and low carbohydrates' plastered across the front are like a glowing beacon. I eat a serving or two of the low-calorie yogurt then immediately throw it back into the fridge before I eat any more.

Okay, that's dinner. But now I need something to help silence the negative voice in my head. As I go to close the fridge door, I see a half empty bottle of vodka staring at me, just waiting to be consumed. *Perfect*. There are no sugar-free mixers in the house but hey, nothing's as sugar free as straight vodka.

It's so nice to have the house all to myself: no judgement about my choices, no one to force me to eat a real, nutritious dinner or stop me from drinking vodka alone in my bedroom. No Mum saying, 'Why won't you just eat it!' or my brother Trent saying,

'You're looking so skinny, mate, it's out of control.' And no lying to myself, *I'm just not hungry* while my rumbling stomach begs for more food.

I sit on my bed, holding my nose and taking swig after swig of vodka until I feel happier. Happiness turns to numbness and then, best of all, sweet oblivion.

9

ROD: 'I gave up my family for you'

I think I've found my Prince Charming. I can imagine a house, a dog, a committed long-term relationship with Adam. His family accepts him, me, us. Our friends are more than okay with us being together and in my head everything is great. Everything except my family.

Even though I told my parents they were dead to me I can't bring myself to stop speaking to them altogether. The problem is, every time I speak to them, it just turns into an argument. They tell me that this is a phase, that I'll get over it. Mum always tells me that I'm going to get hurt, not realising that she and Dad are the cause of a lot of my pain already.

Not long before my twenty-second birthday my parents get in touch to tell me they have a gift for me. Reluctantly, I head on over. As soon as I step through the door I can feel the tension. I am uncomfortable, they are uncomfortable, and I feel like an outsider in my own family home.

'Happy birthday,' Dad says.

'Happy birthday, darlin,' says Mum, as she leans in for a kiss and a hug but it's cold. I don't know if I am pulling away or whether Mum and Dad are just uncomfortable around me now.

They give me a card and a David Beckham cologne. It's awkward accepting a gift from people I don't even feel comfortable around anymore. Every time we try to have a civil conversation it always ends in a raging fight where both sides say things that can't be taken back.

This time the fight breaks out as I'm leaving and we're standing on the driveway out the front. I'm so angry that I feel like a stranger here that I scream at them at the top of my lungs – every neighbour in the street would've heard every word. I tell them that I don't want or need anything from them anymore and forcefully shove the gift back into Mum's hands.

I speed off down the street, consumed with rage. All I can see is red. I pull over on the side of the road and as typical angry boys do in their early twenties, I have a rant on Facebook. I type the letters F-A-M-I-L-Y and proceed to complete my angry acrostic poem:

F – Fucked; A – Assholes; M – Manipulators; I – Interferes when not wanted; L – Liars; Y – YES, My Family.

I've become a bit of a hothead since I tried to come out at seventeen and have learned to not take shit from anyone. When I get home and take a second to relax, I realise the post is harsh and remove it.

Later that night, Adam and I are already in bed when my housemate, Hayden (not Faith, I've since moved in to a party house) knocks on my door to tell me my family are here. I feel my heart sink, and my mind immediately goes to the Facebook post. I leave Adam in the room and go out to find my brother, brother-in-law and future brother-in-law at the front door. The verbal bombardment begins as soon as I step out.

'We're fucked, are we?'

'What's wrong with you?'

'Why don't you get a girlfriend?'

It goes from bad to worse. I feel attacked and singled out and am struggling to hold it together. It's three against one and I feel really threatened. I turn around to get away from them and go back inside, but the door has locked behind me.

I bang as hard as I can on the door and scream for Hayden to help me – not Adam, as I'm sure his presence would only escalate things further.

'Fuck you, you are not fucking welcome here!' I shout. 'Get the fuck off my property!'

I push them away from me before I get pinned against the wall. Hayden opens the door, tells them they need to go before the police arrive and tries to drag me inside. The boys are heading back to the car, but I'm kicking and screaming and holding onto the door frame so Hayden can't get me inside. I'm consumed with rage like never experienced before.

'How fucking dare they. I hate them so much!' I yell as my housemate pulls me inside and slams the door shut.

As always, the anger quickly softens and turns to sorrow as I collapse in a heap on the floor. I'm crying so hard I can't breathe. I feel like a whole decade of suppressed pain and heartache is coming out of me in this moment. I know this is it: the words I've said to my parents will be the last I speak to any of them.

Even though things haven't been good with my family for some time, now they reach an all-time low. So many family events and parties come and go – birthdays, Mothers' Day, Fathers' Day, Christmas. I don't get invited to any of them.

It seems I'm officially barred from the family.

At least things can't get much worse, I tell myself.

Something doesn't feel right with me and Adam, even though we have been together about a year at this stage. I don't want to be that person who doesn't trust their partner and feels the need to go through their phone but hey, I have to know and I don't think he's being honest with me.

When he's in the shower I decide to peek. His phone password is 1234, real creative. I open his phone and immediately notice a folder with the gay dating app Grindr in it. He's obviously put it inside a folder so I won't see it when he has his phone out around me.

My heart starts beating fast and I get this twisting, sick feeling. I open the messages and feel the colour drain from my face. Nude photos, sex talk, conversations from only days earlier arranging to meet in car parks and public toilets. People asking him if he has a boyfriend, and his reply: 'NO'.

I open his text messages to find a guy thanking him for the blow job he received from Adam earlier today.

My brain cannot handle what I'm seeing. It's not as if we're not having sex – we're humping like rabbits and everything is still so fun and exciting. We're having sex every time we're together, which is almost every day.

Then it hits me.

Adam is having sex with these random men then coming to my place immediately after and having sex with me.

And it doesn't seem to have fazed him in the slightest. He hasn't been acting strange or guilty at all.

As soon as Adam gets out of the shower I confront him.

'Do you have something you want to tell me, Adam?'

'No, why?' he says.

I turn his phone around and hold it up to his face. 'Are you fucking serious?' I yell.

'I didn't meet with all of them,' he says. 'It's just dirty talk when I'm horny.'

Even with blatant evidence on his phone, he denies having actual sex with anyone else but does say he's been fooling around with hand jobs and blow jobs. He admits to being in the wrong and that he 'fucked up', as he puts it. He is so apologetic and promises me he won't do it again.

'I love you so much and don't want to lose you,' he tells me and pleads with me to give him another chance. I hear Mum's voice in my head saying, *You will get hurt.*

All I can think of is how I cut my family out for my own happiness. I chose Adam over my family because I thought he would make me happy and now this is happening. What are my choices? Dump Adam and admit to my family that he hurt me, or stay and give him another chance?

Taking a deep breath I say, 'Okay, but you need to delete Grindr and get a new phone number. Now.' He agrees and promises me he will change.

I pride myself on being a strong person who would never put up with this kind of thing. If it were happening to a friend of mine, I would tell them to run for the hills. *Why can't I take my own advice?*

New phone number, new Adam. Bunches of flowers brought home to me with a beautiful card and my favourite TV series, *Glee*, on DVD. He's trying so hard. I can trust him again, I think.

One night we're lying in bed after the most intense lovemaking session. We're having a cute moment, cuddling, watching some TV, when my phone vibrates. It's a message from an old acquaintance: 'I am sorry to be the bearer of bad news, but Adam is cheating on you.' I immediately feel sick and read on.

'My housemate just got home and said he has just fucked this guy in a public toilet down near the lake. I asked him for a photo, and I'm so sorry to tell you that it's Adam, just thought you had a right to know.'

I don't know what to do. I feel so hurt but in a strange way I think I saw this coming. I pass my phone to Adam and then sit on the side of the bed and wait for his reaction, his excuse. I'm waiting for him to tell me it's a lie. He doesn't. He just says, 'I am so sorry.' So much of me wants him to lie, tell me it didn't happen. This isn't like last time; he's being honest from the get-go.

'Did you use protection at least?' I ask him.

He hangs his head in shame. 'No.'

'Did you fuck him, or did he fuck you?'

'He fucked me.'

All I can think about is the sex we just had. It seemed so intimate and beautiful … but only an hour earlier he was getting fucked by a random, with no protection, in a dirty public toilet of all places.

I feel so gross. I tell him he needs to go and stay at his parents' until I can figure out what I want to do next.

Text message after text message flood in from him over the next couple of days, apologising and asking for my forgiveness. The same old lines and promises that he won't ever do it again.

I'm at work when I notice multiple missed calls from Adam and messages asking me to call him urgently. I go into the lunchroom, close the door and call him. When he answers, I say, 'What, Adam, I'm at work, what do you want?'

Silence.

'Adam, what do you want? I'm busy.'

'I have chlamydia,' he says.

I'm going to be sick. 'What do you mean?'

He tells me that he went and got an STI test after he had sex with the random. The sexual health nurse just called to say he has chlamydia in his throat and ass and dick.

I hang up on him and immediately call the sex health clinic to ask for an emergency appointment. They fit me in straight away and when I turn up they give me a pill and tell me no sex for ten days.

The test comes back positive for chlamydia. I feel so dirty. I've done nothing wrong, been faithful to my partner and I still end up with an STI. (I know now that anyone can get an STI and it doesn't mean you're 'dirty', of course, but that's how I felt at the time.)

I'm so confused. I don't want to go to bed alone at night; I don't even know how to be single. I'm so angry with Adam and yet I miss him.

I confide in a few of my closest friends – they all say he's a bastard and he doesn't deserve me. I keep telling them they don't see the good times we have together and are only thinking of the bad. I can hear myself making excuses for him and know in my heart of hearts that I'm not strong enough to break it off for good.

I take Adam back and tell him this is definitely his last chance. Just like last time, the flowers, gifts and compliments all flow, along with promises that he'll never hurt me again. He says 'I love you' all the time in person and via text. He gets yet another new number to try to prove to me he's serious.

Having sex with Adam has changed, though. It still feels okay when I come, but the connection is gone. I've always had a super high sex drive but now I'm afraid to touch him for fear of catching another STI. All I can picture when we're being intimate is him doing nasty things with someone else. I keep trying to convince myself that things will get better.

One morning, only a couple of weeks after moving into our new rental together, I wake up feeling unwell. My balls are aching, and I feel like I have just been kicked in the nuts. I kiss Adam goodbye as he's leaving for work and tell him I'm not feeling the greatest. I'm busting to pee. There's also a throbbing pain in my lower abdomen, maybe just because I need to pee so bad. I make my way delicately to the toilet, pull my dick out and my knob is bright red with a white substance on the tip. Gross. My dick has never looked like this before, but I'm still busting so begin to pee. The tiniest bit of wee comes out and it's like razor blades coming out of me. I let out a scream and squeeze my dick to stop the stream. I start and stop peeing in increments until I'm done. By now I'm sweating, my hands are clammy, my stomach is cramping and my dick is throbbing.

I get back to my room, pick up my phone and call Adam. 'Be honest with me, you peace of shit!' I yell down the phone as soon as he picks up. He tells me to calm down and asks me what is wrong.

'Have you fucked anyone else? Do not lie to me!'

'No, no, no, I haven't, I promise I haven't,' he says, but I can hear in his voice he's lying to me.

'Why is my dick red, why is there discharge coming from my knob and why am I peeing razor blades, Adam?'

'I have no idea,' he replies.

I get off the phone and make the dreaded call to the sex health clinic again. The nurse asks me for my symptoms and when I tell her she says to come in immediately. I jump in the shower, get ready and head straight in. I arrive and to my embarrassment it's the same nurse as last time.

We go into the examination room and she says, 'You've been a naughty boy, haven't you?' The joke doesn't land.

I drop my pants and she takes a swab from my dick, puts a swab up my ass and another down my throat. I have to pee in a cup, which is painful as all hell, and she takes some blood. She then tells me that results should be back in a day or two.

It is the longest two days of my life. Adam is still denying he has done anything wrong.

We are sitting on the lounge, arguing, when the phone rings. It's the nurse. I put the phone on loudspeaker and she proceeds to tell me that I've tested positive for chlamydia and gonorrhoea and that I need to come back in for treatment immediately. I hang up the phone, grab my keys and look over at Adam. 'Fuck you,' I say and walk out.

Arriving at the clinic for the third time, I am beyond humiliated. The nurse takes me back into the room I've become awfully familiar with. She gives me the same pills I took last time. 'I'm afraid the treatment for gonorrhoea is an injection in the butt cheek and it's not very pleasant,' she says. She gets her equipment ready and pulls out the biggest bloody needle I've ever seen. 'Okay, there's a numbing agent in with it, which'll ease the pain slightly. And three, two, one, slight sting.' She inserts the needle.

Slight sting! Is she serious? It's the most painful injection I've ever received, like she just injected lava directly into my ass. I think I prefer the razor blades coming out my dick. 'All done!' she says. 'Now you can't have sex for ten days and you'll need to come back for secondary tests then.' She adds that I might have a dead butt for a few hours. Great.

Looking back, alarm bells should have gone off from the get-go, but I'd been blinded by what I'd thought was love. But finally I have to face the truth: I am in a committed relationship with a chronic liar, cheater, sex addict, manipulator and sociopath.

From the beginning I'd been insecure, as Adam was the first man that I'd ever had 'proper sex' with. He'd told me he'd only been with a couple of people before me when really I don't think he could remember how many.

When we'd first got together, when texts would pop up on Adam's phone from someone he was seeing before me, they were actually from guys making sexual advances. He'd say he was going to a family thing or hanging with his cousins but ... he wasn't. For some reason I still don't leave him and this pattern of cheating and forgiveness repeats itself, over and over. I get calls and messages all the time from random people telling me they had sex with Adam and didn't know about me. I hear the dating app message alert go off when Adam has secretly downloaded it again and forgets to delete it (which is his MO – download, hook up, delete, repeat). My friends make fake profiles to catch him out and always do. He gives me multiple STIs from having unprotected sex with strangers (luckily the ones you can get rid of).

He reduces me to a piece of shit he can kick around, and I let him. He makes me hate myself again. He used to be apologetic and accept blame and responsibility but over the last two years that changes. He blames me. He tells me that I didn't bottom enough for him but ironically enough he doesn't complain about the complete strangers that he has to bottom for. He accuses me of talking to other guys, which I'm not, just to give himself an excuse to cheat.

Adam tells the guys he has sex with who do know about me that I'm physically abusive; he says to others we're in an open relationship. He's a compulsive liar. One day his dad has a talk with me and tells me that Adam's young and should be out experimenting – a concept I'm completely okay with if you're not claiming to be in a committed relationship.

I'm totally miserable and I turn to food, alcohol and party drugs to numb me. I gain a lot of weight, which only makes me feel worse. I'm in a dark place and feel I don't have anyone who genuinely loves me. I do, I just can't see it in this moment, and I continue the vicious cycle. I break it off, then take him back and repeat.

I wish I could find the strength to end it and move on. But I don't.

Finally, Adam is the one who moves on. He finds himself a new boyfriend whose life he can destroy.

After everything he has put me through, *he* leaves *me*!

I'm blown away that he just jumps into another relationship. This sends me even further into despair and my self-worth is reduced to nothing.

Mitch steps up and becomes the very best friend a person can ask for. Adam moves out and Mitch moves into the spare room and becomes the new boyfriend, without the sex. We have dinners together, have cosy nights and then party up a storm together on weekends. He takes so much of the pain away.

My phone rings and I see it's Dad calling. I haven't spoken to Dad in months. I don't know what to do. I'm in a good mood today and don't want another fight so I let it ring out. I get a text saying, 'Call me back.' I walk into Mitch's room and he says, 'Just ring back, I'll be right by your side. You can always hang up if it goes bad.'

I take his advice. 'You called,' I say coldly when Dad answers.

'Look mate, I know things haven't been great between us but I thought you needed to know. Your mum's been diagnosed with bone cancer in her femur and is going in for surgery to try to remove it at the end of next week.'

'What do you mean?' I muster.

'If you'd like to come round, we'd like to see you and we can fill you in,' says Dad.

I get off the phone. Mitch gives me a big hug. I drive myself over to my parents' house feeling numb.

Entering their estate brings a sense of dread. I knock on the door – even this is strange as I'd always just let myself in. Now I feel like a guest.

Mum lets me in. I kiss her on the cheek. 'How have you been?' she asks.

'Really good, Mum,' I lie.

We walk into the kitchen where Dad's standing and he gives me a kiss too. My pop had always taught us not to be ashamed of kissing your dad. Dad offers me a drink and we all go outside to their entertaining area by the pool. This feels much more relaxed than the bloody lounge inside that's hosted so many awkward conversations in the past.

'So what's going on, Mum?' I start. I'm so concerned about her so I jump right in. And there's no way I'm having another 'gay' chat or telling them about Adam.

Mum outlines what she's been through in recent months dealing with symptoms, trying to get a diagnosis and finally discovering that it was cancer. I feel terrible that I've missed it all. The surgery will be major; they basically have to remove her femur by cutting near the knee and hip. They then need to take the femur out, put it under high levels of radiation and reattach it to the body with bolts, plates and screws.

I stay for an hour or so and ask Mum if she minds if I come to Sydney to be with her before her surgery. She tells me, 'I would love that.' Although we're far from mending our relationship, for now we call a truce as I need to be there for her.

The surgery goes well. Six months later, her scans come back clear, but her full recovery takes much longer. As far as our relationship goes, we're fine and I'm getting along with the family as long as we continue not to utter the big scary 'gay' word. It feels like I'll never have the freedom to be myself – if I even know who that is.

I am still partying hard (because Mitch is a big party boy, too) and it is a great distraction but things begin to feel a bit hollow. I want to get away, clear my head, do something for someone else. The decisions I've been making – from drinking, drugs and partying way too much – are toxic and only getting me into trouble. I need to sort myself out.

As I'm scrolling through Facebook, I come across a girl I used to go to church with. She has posted these magnificent photos of herself in Uganda, East Africa, where she's been volunteering to help underprivileged kids, and what I see makes my heart happy. *I want to do that.* I start researching volunteering opportunities and quickly notice that most of the organisations are Christian. *That's okay*, I think, *it'll only be for a short period, then I'll come back to my life.*

Within four weeks I arrive in Kampala, the capital of Uganda, feeling like I'm on another planet. I'm immediately hit with the dry heat and an unfamiliar, sweaty, smoky smell. The airport is run-down, there's hardly any security and I realise very quickly that I stand out like a sore thumb as I'm one of the few white people – 'mzungu' in the local Bantu language. The director of the aid organisation, Belinda, is waiting to pick me up from the airport and she escorts me to a white mini-van that will take us the 70 kilometres west to Mityana, which is more of a village than a town, and the roads are dusty and bumpy. We drive past homes that are tiny huts or sheets of tin held up with tree branches, entire families living in shelters smaller than my bedroom.

The heat is intense and there's a pungent smell in the dry air which Belinda tells me is sewage or waste. She explains they don't have a good sewerage system; most people don't have proper toilets and there's no waste management – everyone just burns their rubbish. That was the smell that hit me on arrival.

We get to the house we're staying at and are met at the gate by our very own armed guard. The gates open and a bunch of kids run up to greet me. These kids, a lot of whom are orphans, have the biggest smiles on their faces and greet me with hugs as though they've known me their entire lives. The kids direct me down a dirt track to a guesthouse at the back of the property with a magnificent view of the plains, which are filled with baobab trees – it's like a scene straight from *The Lion King*.

The house itself is comfortable and nothing like the houses we'd passed on the way from the airport.

The next day we head out to what is essentially a slum. Sewage runs into a flowing creek, then kids downstream are lapping the water out of their hands. It's hard to see human beings living this way and it really puts into sharp perspective how lucky I am to have grown up in Newcastle.

In the afternoon, we go to the local soccer field, where the village soccer team is competing against a nearby village. It's just a dirt pitch and a stand made of tree branches bound together. We walk through the grounds and find our spot in the stand. We hear 'Mzungu, mzungu' being muttered around us. Some of these people have never met or even seen a white person. Some hiss at us in repulsion, some just want to touch us and others beg for money. For our own safety we don't stay too long.

My job on this trip is to teach English to the kids. I also do school pick-up and drop-off, which means piling about twenty kids into the back of a ute or into a mini-van. I pick up pig feed, help in the field with the crops, cook and clean. It's certainly not glamorous, but I can feel this trip changing my outlook. I have a new appreciation for the life I have at home. The people here don't have much but seem to manage without complaint and with a smile.

The kids continually question me about whether I am married or have a girlfriend, and I always answer, 'Not yet.' I attend church and am even asked to preach one day, which strangely enough I'm able to do quite easily, even though I'm conscious that I'm putting on an act.

Towards the end of my six weeks in Uganda, we are taken to a babies' orphanage, where I meet two baby boys who I just fall in love with immediately. The woman running the home tells me that these two boys are very hard to settle, and they cry all the time. She hands them both to me and I sit there with one in each arm. They cuddle into me and both fall asleep. After we leave, I can't get these boys out of my mind. Something inside of me wants to help them, but how?

In what seems like no time at all I have to leave Uganda. I cry all the way home on the plane, reading the letters all the kids have written to me and thinking about those two baby boys.

Back at home, I have zero interest in dating, partying or anything really. I just want to go back to Uganda. I want to do more to help those baby boys than just sponsoring them.

I get back in touch with the aid organisation and tell them I want to adopt the boys. They provide me with information on the steps I need to follow, and it's much harder than I could have imagined. First, I have to live in Uganda with the boys in my care for three years before being allowed to start the adoption process and leave the country. The next big issue is that it's illegal to be gay in Uganda; in fact, if you're found to be gay, you'll likely be murdered and the police will turn a blind eye. I was okay with hiding my sexuality for my six-week volunteering holiday, but three years is a long time.

I think about it for a while and I decide not to be selfish. No one had a clue I was gay on the first trip, I have no temptation in Uganda – sex hardly crossed my mind – and I need to do something to help those little boys.

The next time I go around to my parents' house, I sit Mum and Dad down and let them know my plans, which they are hesitantly excited about.

'Does this mean you've given your life back over to God, Rod?' Mum asks with a hopeful look on her face.

'Are you not into boys anymore?' Dad wants to know.

I don't know what to tell them. I don't want to lie. I say, 'I don't know, I can't just turn that off you know.'

The mood in the room changes. 'What are you going to do? Live in Uganda, adopt these boys, bring them home then settle down with a bloke?' says Dad. 'That's not right, you can't do that.'

Here we go again. Every single time the gay topic comes up it ends in a fight.

'Does the organisation know you like boys?' Mum asks me.

'No!' I reply.

And then comes the confrontation, like it always does. This time it's: 'Unless you can tell us that you're not gay, and that you've recommitted your life to God, unfortunately we're going to have to tell the organisation and you won't be going,' she says.

I can't believe it. I sit there enraged but then something occurs to me. My intentions are pure but what would following through on my plan do to me? I've lived a lie for so long and now I'm about to do it all over again. Even though it breaks my heart to admit it, this isn't the right move for me. I tell Mum and Dad I won't go and they offer to sponsor one of the boys, which is kind of them.

I'm now more confused than ever about my direction in life. I feel so lost.

A typical day at our favourite beach, One Mile Beach, Port Stephens, mucking around. The fewer clothes the better in summer. (*Andrew Simington*)

(Rod) From not a care in the world to being halfway out trying to hold on to what 'straight' parts of me I had left. With siblings Kelly, Matt and Emma when I was 18.

(Tim) Do you think my two older brothers might have had an inkling I was gay? I was always so quirky and different to my brothers but so desperately wanted to fit in, including by drinking beers, which I never really liked. That's me with Mum, Trent and Ben. And I'm on the steps with my dad, Rocko, on my first day of kindergarten. Best mates, always.

LOOKING FOR OURSELVES

(Rod) Escaping my life in Australia to volunteer in Uganda when I was 23, teaching English and generally just helping out a community with great heart but no money. I was trying to bridge my Christian world and gay self and became closeted all over again.

(Tim) Outta Hollywood maybe, but not so STRAIGHT. It felt so liberating being in West Hollywood, the only place I felt I could be myself. Top right, I'm in front of the Canadian Rockies, where I worked at a resort. I'm most likely still drunk from the night before and hiding from the girl I attempted to lose my virginity to.

You're not boyfriends unless you wear matching hats, apparently. Here we are on a cruise a few months into our relationship; we befriended a pole-dancing convention and were known as 'the dancing boys'. Buoyed by these efforts, we went to an Ariana Grande concert dressed up as her backing dancers and got half-price drinks all night (and posed for pics with many fans, who may well be disappointed if they see this). Bottom right, we were white-water rafting in Bali. That night, we said 'I love you' for the first time.

Out and proud, advocating for Marriage Equality. And Tim celebrating on One Mile Beach, Port Stephens, the scene of some incredible highs as well as his absolute rock bottom.

(Rod) After an elaborate set-up, which I still can't believe he didn't twig, Tim came through our house saying 'don't scare me'. It wasn't until he saw fairy lights, and a trail of rose petals leading to me standing under a flower archway and wearing a suit, that he realised what was really about to happen. Then he said 'YES'!

Our wedding ceremony set up on One Mile Beach, Port Stephens. One of the best things about our day was that loads of strangers, just regular beachgoers, stopped and celebrated two men exchanging vows. (*Vision Collective*)

(Rod) Mum and Dad walking me down the aisle, after all we had been through. They were gripping my hands so tight; they must have been so nervous. We all were, but the hurt began to melt away with those few steps. *(Vision Collective)*

(Tim) Kathy, my mum and the rock for so much of my life, walking me down the aisle. *(Vision Collective)*

I now pronounce you Husbands. Our first kiss as an officially married couple, in front of 100 of our closest family and friends. We couldn't have asked for more. *(Vision Collective)*

(Rod) Mother and Son dance at our reception. Our relationship has been to hell and back, and this moment meant more to me than anyone could ever imagine. *(Vision Collective)*

Never did we think only months later we would become 'The Newlyweds' on *The Amazing Race Australia* and be the first same-sex married couple on Australian reality television ... SPOILER ALERT — the Gay Team wins! *(Vision Collective)*

Top left: Checking into the Pitstop on the border between North and South Korea, after completing a military bootcamp and kayaking down the rapids.

Top right: Ripping open a clue and getting ready to race out of the airport in Zimbabwe, Africa, after getting a traditional welcome from an elder who spat water in our faces.

Bottom left: Wading through a swamp in Vietnam, trying to collect 100 snails so we could get the next clue. We are laughing because Tim stacked it and our sound crew was having a conniption because his mic got wet.

'Tim and Rod, you are the winners of *The Amazing Race Australia*.'

A moment we had dreamed of our whole lives. Not winning *The Amazing Race* specifically, but being successful and celebrated for being our true selves. Never give up on you; you just don't know when things are going to click.

Our family: Tim, Diesel and Rod. We will settle for a fur baby until we are ready for our own human. Nothing makes us happier than our boy Diesel.

10

TIM: Super drunk and horny

It's Saturday night and I'm getting ready to head to a friend's 21st. I'm trying to make an effort, not cut myself off completely, and 21st birthday parties are my favourite events because everyone's wasted so I won't have to fear the awkward sober social anxiety. Plus, the theme tonight is 'Superhero' and I'll never miss an opportunity to dress up and express myself as my confident and courageous alter ego. I'm excited about wearing my Superman costume. True, I would much prefer to go as Catwoman, but that would obviously scream GAY – not what I want people to be thinking!

I've been told there will be an open bar but the social anxiety has already kicked in and I know if I don't quickly skol a few drinks before I leave, I'll be an anxious mess when I arrive. My voice will shake and I'll be obviously trembling. That would be total social suicide and is a million per cent not an option.

I make my way to the kitchen and quietly sneak out some sugar-free premixed drinks I hid at the back of the family fridge earlier today. I don't want to make it obvious to Mum that I have a problem or that there's anything she needs to worry about.

Back in my room I close the door behind me, being as careful as possible not to clink the bottles together as I move. As I start skoling the drinks, I instantly feel all the worry, fear and stress miraculously evaporate from my body. I sense that this is wrong, but I don't care. People seem to like me more and I feel like I am a lot more confident and funnier when I am intoxicated.

After finishing all four drinks and hiding the empty bottles under a mountain of clothes in my cupboard, I'm ready to leave. All my friends drink, but I'm conscious that I need to hide the fact that I'm reliant on it. I've got really good at finding a level of intoxication where people don't know I'm drunk, which helps me slide under the radar.

I especially don't want Mum to notice me slurring my words while I'm in the car with her – that would be like having I HAVE BEEN DRINKING ALONE tattooed across my forehead. So I try my hardest to maintain a convincing sober demeanour and Mum drops me off at the party with no inkling I am intoxicated, FANTASTIC.

My friend's place is a big two-storey brick house, and every window is lit up. The place is heaving. Aussie hip-hop is blaring out into the suburban night, only just holding its own against a wall of voices, laughing, shrieking, yelling. I shiver and pull my Superman cape around myself. I'm suddenly freezing and the buzz from my pre-drinks has disappeared. *Open bar*, I tell myself. *Get in there and find that open bar.*

A few people I know from my school approach me and begin

making small talk. I can immediately feel the social anxiety pouring back into my body. *OMG you didn't drink enough before you left.* I'm trapped in the mindset of my younger self. I didn't know who could be at the party so assumed the worst: that maybe some bullies from my childhood would reappear to torment me all over again.

I force some very awkward and uncomfortable fake smiles then quickly excuse myself and head in the direction of the bathroom. I just need a few minutes alone to wait until this tremendous wave of anxiety passes. On the way to the bathroom, I see a fridge filled with every beer imaginable, calling to me like a beacon. Gross, I don't even like beer but it has alcohol in it so it'll do. I quickly grab two beers, as if I'm also grabbing a drink for my non-existent friend, and then lock myself in the bathroom. I crack the bottle tops off both beers and skol them as quickly as possible, difficult because I don't like it but I hold my nose and chug them both down like a thirsty elephant. The bottles are empty in a matter of seconds.

There's a knock at the door, soon followed by multiple, pounding knocks. Someone is busting. Flustered, I hide the empty bottles behind the toilet and yell, 'One more second, sorry!'

As I slink out of the bathroom, I once again feel a surge of happiness and confidence. I can't wait to get drunker. Straight back to the beer-filled fridge I go and steadily drink myself into oblivion.

You'll be alone forever. Your family and friends won't want anything to do with you. People will think you're disgusting.

Despite my best efforts to drown it out with alcohol, calorie deprivation and exercise, the voice in my head is louder than ever. After what feels like a lifetime of internal struggle, I have finally come to terms with accepting myself for who I truly am. I am gay. And my inner saboteur is not happy about it.

Overshadowing everything is an immense fear of what my life will look like now. I have an extremely negative perception of what my future gay existence will be. I am scared of what people will think of me for being Gay and cannot stop wondering if everyone will be able to accept it.

How will I find a partner, have a successful career and potentially one day build a happy family as a gay man? Growing up, real-life gay role models have been non-existent and even in the media I see little to no representation of successful and happy gay men. The only gay people I've been exposed to are in movies and television, and they're not the type of person I relate to or feel like. The gay men I see portrayed in the media are usually very flamboyant and overtly feminine. They always seem to be a flight attendant or hairdresser and love to sleep with hundreds of men. They're never settled down or seem happy in a monogamous relationship, and they always seem to be nasty and mean-spirited. This stereotype confuses me because I don't fit it, even though I'm Gay.

I don't want to sleep around like every other gay person I know of. I just want a loving relationship with someone who shares the same values and accepts me for me. Not being able to relate to anyone like myself makes me feel so alone and afraid. I feel as though no matter how far and wide I search, there's no one out there like me.

I'm so incredibly stressed out about being gay and people finding out, that I'm getting on my own nerves. If I had to rate my current anxiety and stress level, I'd say it's close to 2007 Britney: I feel like I've been pushed so far that at any given time I could have a meltdown and severely beat a car with an umbrella.

Whenever I feel anxious, which is all time, I turn to alcohol. It's my new best friend who's always there for me. We don't just hang out on weekends anymore – no, we spend every day together. When I'm drunk, I'm truly numb to all the worry and pressure. It offers me a fleeting moment of happiness where I can escape into a world of liberation and self-love. I don't hate myself; I'm almost proud and excited for what life will bring me and who I want to eventually become. The only problem is, I can't stay drunk forever and when I sober up, the fear and anxiety come racing back and begin controlling me all over again. I am stuck in a never-ending spiral, becoming weaker and weaker as I drink more, eat less and furiously exercise.

I'm still living rent-free at our family home in Newcastle and working at the local hotel – as many shifts as possible, in fact, because I'm desperate to save money and run away to America forever. I think that if I go to America all my dreams will come true and my troubles will magically melt away.

I'm twenty-two at this stage. Ben and Trent have both moved out, got married and are starting families of their own. Dad's still living in our holiday house in Port Stephens, where he moved after he and Mum separated. This leaves Mum and me in the four-bedroom house together. Mum works a lot, which allows me to lock myself away and hide from the world most days. I spend countless hours shut up in my room, scrolling through Instagram to escape my loneliness.

I only have the courage to interact with gay men online and Instagram is the perfect platform to get validation, and even feel wanted and desired by the community I so desperately crave to be a part of. I'm at least feeling better about my body from all the exercise and weight training I've been doing, thank Christ, and I find that putting sexy photos of myself on Instagram allows me to rebel against my past, and be as gay and as sexy as I want.

Not long after I start posting sexy photos my followers explode to a whole new level. I'm going up thousands of followers each day and can't believe how amazing it makes me feel! Like Kim Kardashian when she got her ass out on the cover of *Paper* magazine and broke the internet.

I'm finally being accepted and almost celebrated for being gay. *This is my moment*, I think, and I devote myself to being as suggestive as humanly possible in order to make these complete strangers horny. The likes and comments are like a drug and before I know it I'm officially addicted, pushing the boundaries of what's acceptable in order to get my hit of social media validation.

Out in the day-to-day world, it's a very different story. Somehow I'm still studying a Bachelor of Business at uni, but meeting new people, group assignments and class presentations all give me terrible social anxiety.

Driving to uni on the day of a major presentation, I'm actually terrified – I can see my hands visibly shaking on the steering wheel. My throat's dry, I have an enormous pit in my stomach and my heart is beating like crazy. I make a quick turn into a bottle shop and pick up the cheapest bottle of wine I can find. When I get to uni I pull into the back of the parking area, under the shade of a tree, far away from any other cars. I put on my favourite song, Katy Perry's 'California Girls', turn it right up to try to calm my nerves and, hopefully, help me build up the courage to speak in front of the class. It doesn't work. I can feel myself getting more and more anxious as the clock on the dash ticks closer and closer to my presentation time.

Plan B. I reach over and grab the bottle of wine from the back seat. It's early and I have a full day of classes ahead before I need to drive home, so I can have a few glasses of wine. I rip the lid off and start skolling straight from the bottle. It feels like I've opened the floodgates. *One more sip* is followed by *Just one more sip* and before I know it the bottle's empty. I have drunk every drop. Now I just need to pull myself together.

As I make my way to class, I can feel the alcohol really starting to kick in. I've drunk way too much, but there's no turning back now. I walk into the classroom and see my name written at the

139

top of the list on the white board: I am going first. With the alcohol under my belt, my nerves are totally gone; my mission now is to conceal that I'm heavily intoxicated.

When I stand up in front of the large group, I feel like I have all the confidence in the world and my presentation skills are incredible. I breeze through, and as I wrap it up, I almost don't want it to end. I feel so powerful and in control of this moment and so free from all my previous anxiety and fear.

As soon as I sit back down, I start thinking ahead to my other presentations coming up in the next few weeks. I begin to concoct ways I can get intoxicated before them without anyone knowing. I feel like I've cracked the Da Vinci code and discovered the key to university success – in order to feel in control, powerful and confident I just need to skol a bottle of wine alone in my car before every presentation.

Before long I'm getting drunk multiple times a week before going to class. I don't even need to have a presentation as an excuse and find myself drinking alone before any random lecture or a tutorial. Alcohol and I are the perfect companions, more iconic than Bert and Ernie, Batman and Robin, even Scooby Doo and Shaggy.

Alcohol helps me cope with the bullshit that's going on in my head. It helps me see a happy gay future on the horizon filled with rainbows and unicorns. So I'm happy to put up with the negative consequences that come with my drinking. Even though I have severe hangovers, blackouts and vomit all the time

I still don't want to stop. Life is just so much better when I'm drunk.

One of my favourite things to do is go to my local beach at night, sit on the sand and blast iconic gay anthems on my iPod Shuffle while I drink by myself. One hot summer's night in December I walk to my favourite beach, sit myself down at the far end with a backpack full of UDLs, and put on my headphones.

The sand becomes cold on my bare feet as the sun disappears behind the sand dunes. Before long a full moon lights up the entire empty beach. It's like I'm marooned on a desert island with just the drinks in my bag and my gay playlist. The millions of stars are so bright I feel like I can see into infinity.

But suddenly, for some reason I snap out of my fantasy. I'm overcome with rage at being gay and so fearful of future judgement for being this way. Tears start falling, and I just can't bear to be where I am, who I am, feeling how I do a moment longer. I push away the can, drop my iPod in the sand and wade into the water fully clothed, towards the waves crashing out past the shallows.

As I make my way further away from the shore the waves begin to break against my body. Salt water splashes up into my face and washes my tears away. As I look out to the horizon, I can see the full moon glowing above the eerie ocean, almost calling me to swim further out to sea. My feet can no longer touch the sand and I begin to dive through the surf.

Would anyone really miss me? Should I just put myself out of this misery and drown myself right here and now? In this moment I'm so tired of living this way and I just want the pain to stop. I am feeling so defeated that drowning seems like my best option. Bobbing in the cold water, unable to stop my tears, I'm ready to let it all go.

I think of my family and how much I love them. And then I start to think about how my actions will affect them. *I can't do this to them.* Deep down I know this isn't the answer to my pain.

I turn around and begin swimming as fast I can back to shore. When my feet touch sand again I drag myself out of the water, in a state of shock. I lie there on the beach gasping, my body drained of all its tears, totally spent. In the process, I've somehow been able to grasp onto an ounce of hope. There's now a tiny part of me that is slightly optimistic about what could be a happy future.

I go on to finish my degree, and then I begin a three-year Leadership Training Program at Woolworths, which starts with store management skills at my local Woolies. When I start my second year, I move to Sydney, into a small three-bedroom apartment in Meadowbank right next to the trainline, sharing with two other graduates in the program.

I've become good mates with a guy from work and go over to his house for beers one Saturday night. I still hate beer but when I'm around other guys, I feel pressure to drink it to look straighter – what I wouldn't give to be sipping on a pink Vodka Cruiser through a straw. The night starts out as any normal mates' hangout would, with us drinking copious amounts of beer while playing snooker and darts, but the drunker we get the more flirtatious we both become. We've never spoken about our sexuality before; he doesn't know I'm gay and I've always just assumed he's completely straight. Every time he passes me to take his shot, he's getting super close and basically presses his entire body against mine. I catch him looking me up and down with a glimmer of seduction in his eye. When we're sitting next to each other outside after a game he subtly caresses my leg. He leans his head so close to mine when we're in deep conversation, almost to the point where our lips are going to be touching. All of this is making me incredibly horny.

This has taken me by surprise. As we sit side by side, totally wasted in his backyard, we make the most intense eye contact. I've never experienced a connection like this before. It's the first time in my life I'm turned on by a man and at the same time he's looking back at me with the same intensity and emotion. Before I can second-guess the moment, he puts his hand at the back of my head and kisses me passionately. An entire lifetime of worry, stress and confusion seems to just melt away instantly. We jump up and basically sprint into his bedroom, where we strip each other's clothes off faster than a lightning bolt. We begin rolling around on his bed together totally naked, like two dogs on heat. I'd thought I'd be so worried and scared during my first-ever sexual experience with a man but I'm not. I am just super drunk and horny.

The sensation of a man's hands and lips all over my body is everything I've been longing for all these years. My heart is racing with excitement as we explore every part of each other's body. This is exactly what my heart desires. I can't believe how incredibly lucky I am to finally have a naked man on top of me. I feel like I've just won *Who Wants to be a Millionaire*. Everything I've been secretly craving for years is now happening. I am sucking on a man's penis for the first time and having mine sucked in return. I have someone else's fingers inside of me for the first time and it feels great. As he lies on top of me, I wrap my legs around him and our bodies intertwine. I know what's about to happen. This is the part where he slides his penis inside of me. This is going to be my first time having anal sex. I'm not even nervous or scared, just incredibly excited and completely into it. We have what seems like hours of fooling around, eating ass and sucking dick and ass penetration, and afterwards we kiss each other good night and pass out.

I wake up the next morning and instantly recall what happened last night. I replay in my head everything that took place— or at least what I can remember. It feels so natural and normal to me. There's not one part of me that feels regret or sadness or wishes I'd done this with a woman. I jump in my car and drive home blasting Ariana Grande's song 'Break Free' on repeat. This is a monumental moment for me because I truly feel like the experience has allowed me to break free and be my true authentic self to the world. I scream the lyrics as loud as I can while crying happy tears. I feel so liberated. I am definitely gay, and one day I want to fall in love and live happily ever after. While I know that it won't be with this guy from work but I do know my soulmate is out there; I just need to find him.

I am sure this positive first sexual experience with a man has saved my life. It helps give me the power to be honest with the world about who I really am.

I know it's time to be truthful and tell my family and friends about my sexuality.

Coming out to my family is still the most terrifying thing I can imagine. I feel, and hope, that they'll still love and support me, but I just don't want to let them down or for their perception of me to change in a negative way.

Mum has always been a ray of sunshine in my life and I want her to be the very first person I confide in. She's so approachable and understanding, and has stood by me through thick and thin. It might sound corny but she's always taught me that the meaning of life truly is to spread love wherever you go. I know that if anyone is going to reassure me that I've done the right thing by being honest, it'll be Mum. I actually wonder if she already knows. I mean, if me desperately wanting to be in the school's dance troupe, sewing my own *High School Musical* costumes and wanting Britney Spears' latest album for Christmas didn't give it away, I don't know what would. Maybe she's been waiting until

I come to terms with it myself. It is something I need to share with the world on my terms, honestly and directly, and now is the time.

I'm now in the second year of my course living in Sydney, and I decide to take a peaceful afternoon walk one day along the waterfront near where I live. I'm completely sober so therefore pretty anxious at the thought of telling Mum, but something in my heart says it's time to get it off my chest. I think it'll be a lot easier to express my feelings without looking at Mum; that's my theory anyway. I dial her number but only let it ring once or twice, then freak out and hang up. I do that a couple of times and the third time she answers right away. My heart stops. The palm of my phone hand is very sweaty, and I keep asking Mum meaningless questions to divert the conversation from what I am actually calling to tell her. After my multiple questions she finally asks, 'And how are you, my darling son?' That's when I burst into tears. By this time, I've walked into the local dog park and I'm surrounded by people and their pooches. I don't care.

'Is everything okay?' she asks, her voice full of concern.

'Yes, Mum, I'm fine, but there's something I need to tell you …'

There's dead silence as the tears continue to roll down my cheeks and onto the phone. This is it. *There's no turning back now.* I'm finding it much harder than I'd expected. If anyone is going to love me for me, I know it's my beautiful mum. Regardless, I'm terrified of the ramifications of what I'm about to say.

Mum can hear me crying and fills the silence: 'I love you, Tim, you know you can tell me anything.'

This gives me strength. I take a big deep breath and say, 'I am gay.'

Without any hesitation, Mum replies, 'I love you forever and always and I am so proud of the man that you are.'

Instantly I feel a huge weight lift off my shoulders. Mum continues, 'It takes courage to be yourself and I am so proud that you've been able to be so open and honest. Tim, I love you to the stars and back and all I want for you is to be happy.'

I knew Mum would be supportive, but she has just gone above and beyond with her love and kindness. *Every gay man deserves a mother like mine*, I think. I feel so fortunate to have her warm, beautiful presence in my life. I hang up, sit back on the grass, and feel a huge wave of unconditional love flood through my body. Not only for Mum but also – for the first time in a long time – for myself.

Next, I need to tell my brothers.

That weekend I head up to Lennox Head, a beachside town on the north coast of New South Wales, to visit my brothers and their families. Ben recently became a father and everyone else's going to visit. It's such a laidback place, you can hear the waves breaking wherever you are. Every second person seems to be in a wetsuit and carrying a surfboard either on their way to or from the beach. This is the perfect opportunity to tell my brothers in person, and I'm so nervous.

My brothers and I are close but different in so many ways. I know they love me, but I'm scared they'll have an issue with me being gay. They've never had any gay friends that I know of and even the word 'gay' has negative connotations for them. 'That's so gay', 'Don't be a homo' and 'What a fucking faggot' are all slurs I heard flying around among my brothers and their friends as a kid, and I believe that this is the way they still think. During the seven-hour drive north, I play positive and negative scenarios in my head of how they might react. I'm keen to tell them at the first opportunity.

Mum's running around frantically tidying up and my brothers are sitting on the back veranda relaxing while they enjoy an ice-cold afternoon beer. Ben and Trent decide to go for a drive to check out the surf and also call in at the bottle-o and grab a few more beers for the night. They round everyone up and we jump in the car and make the journey down to the locals' secret surf spot.

Ben's driving, Trent's riding shotgun and I'm squashed next to my niece Poppy's car seat in the back. My heart is racing. We pull at the beach carpark and Trent jumps out for a quick swim. I'm suddenly alone in the car with Ben. I take a deep breath. I pull out my phone and show my brother a YouTube video I found a few weeks ago, a short clip of a father who takes his young son to a toy store and lets him buy whatever toy he wants. The son returns with a mermaid doll and then the father praises him for being himself, encouraging his son to be whoever he wants to be, and promises to love and accept him no matter what life he chooses to live. The video really resonated with me and seeing my brother is now a dad, I think it may resonate with him as well.

When it ends, I turn to my brother and say, 'How cool is that dad, he loves his kid no matter what.'

My brother looks at me with genuine love in his eyes. 'I want you to know I feel the same way about you, mate,' he says. 'No matter who you are or what you choose to do in life, I'll always support you.'

I let out a huge breath I didn't know I was holding. The relief is enormous. My brother has just created a space for me to finally be honest with him.

'I want to tell you I'm gay, mate,' I say.

My brother leans over and grabs me in a huge hug. 'We all love you for you, mate, and want you to be happy. Nothing has changed for me and you'll always be my brother who I love and support.'

I could not be happier in this moment. I tell Trent later that afternoon. We're having drinks by the pool in the warm afternoon sun when I find myself alone with Trent and show him the video. He has a similar response to Ben and after giving me a huge hug he showers me with love and acceptance. As the sun begins to set, I realise that my dad is the only person left to tell. This is going to be the hardest one of all.

Dad is the epitome of a typical 'Aussie bloke'. He loves watching horse racing on weekends, enjoys every sport under the sun and is always drinking truckloads of beer with his mates. If I had to paint a picture of what kind of person my dad is, it would be a mixture of Crocodile Dundee and Steve Irwin. I've always been scared shitless of letting him down, especially as Ben and Trent always seem like an impossible act to follow. I'm afraid that being myself will humiliate Dad and make him feel I've disgraced the entire family.

A little while after my trip to Lennox Head, I'm spending the weekend at Mum's in Newcastle and decide to go up to Port Stephens to tell Dad. It's a beautiful sunny day but the forty-five minute drive is torturous. I keep playing a coming-out script in my head over and over. The radio's turned off and the windows are up, I don't want any distractions. I need to be in the right headspace for this otherwise I feel like at any given moment I could turn the car around and drive straight home.

But I keep thinking of how positive he always is with me. He tells me he loves me multiple times a day. When I hang up the phone from him, when I leave his house, he always says, 'I love you, best mate', which makes me feel great. He is a legend, but deep down it scares the hell out of me. *Will he love me as much when I tell him I'm gay?*

As I get closer to Dad's house, I see the huge sand dunes through the trees.

I pull up out the front and make my way to the front door, dragging my heels.

'Legend! Good to see you, mate!' Dad says. 'Hurry up and get inside before the bloody flies come in.' He offers me a tinnie. It's beer but I eagerly crack it open and sit down on the couch next to him.

Still teetering on the brink of running out the door and going back to Newcastle, I dig deep. A sudden burst of courage nudges me over the line. Looking around at all the framed photographs Dad has of me and my brothers at various stages, I say, 'Dad, I'm gay.'

Dead silence fills the room. I swear I can hear my heartbeat echoing through the house.

OMG what have I done? I sneak a look at Dad.

He is tearing up and then a proud smile appears on his face and he pulls me into a loving and supportive hug. He looks me in the eyes and, wiping away his tears, says, 'Mate, I love you so much, you are my hero and I just want you to be happy, legend.'

A feeling of acceptance washes over me, and in what feels like a release of pure happiness I burst into tears as well. By now Dad has me in a full-blown headlock, and is repeatedly kissing me on the forehead and telling me over and over how much he loves me. Then he says in his true-blue comic fashion, 'Mate, I don't care if you bring home a one-eyed alien as long as you're happy.' This outrageous statement is Dad to a tee, and it means the world to me.

My family could not have handled my coming out any better and I'm so grateful to have them all in my life. The fact that they showered me with nothing but love, support and acceptance from the moment I told them I was gay is a testament to their character. I wish the world had more accepting and open-minded families like mine.

This feeling of being wholly accepted and loved is the purest joy I've ever experienced. As it sinks in that I can finally be honest with everyone about who I truly am, a lot of my inner hate stops. I don't rely on alcohol as much; now when I drink it's to have fun and laugh with others and not to numb myself. In a way I feel like I've been reborn. With this new sense of inner pride and acceptance, I'm determined to make my future a bright one, find love, true happiness and conquer the world. Bring it on!

11

ROD: The ultimate revenge sex

At some point in life, you may go through what I've discovered to be the ten stages of a break-up.

In most cases it starts with SHOCK; that is, if you didn't see it coming a mile away and weren't holding onto something that inevitably was going to fail. Yes, that's me.

Then, when you decide to let yourself feel, you progress to the stage we all hate and that is PAIN, more commonly known as HEARTBREAK. Heartbreak has to be one of the worst types of pain you can feel.

As the pain starts to ease, let me introduce you to Mr CONFUSION. He is responsible for the self-doubt, sleepless nights and voices in your head asking, *What did I do wrong? What could I have done differently? Is it my fault?* You'll have a clear mind and a sense of clarity and then Mr Confusion comes knocking again. It's a very frustrating stage.

The next stage is brutal: DENIAL. Here we have the all-too-common bitching with your friends about your ex swiftly followed when you're alone again by you convincing yourself that it's not over. You look for some way to justify your actions or the mistakes of your ex. It's the stage where deep down you know it's over but you cannot let go of the hope you might get back together. I have spent a lot of time here.

Luckily, I stayed strong the last time and continued the journey to the next stage, REFLECTION. This is the part where you stop and really look back at the relationship you had. You reflect on the good times and the bad. For example, I ask myself, *Why the hell did I want him back?*

Number six is where you really start to lose your mind a little bit. It's Mr Confusion on steroids. This is ANGER! You forget any of the good times and focus on the bad. You begin to hate the person you once loved. It's just like in *Mean Girls* when Lindsay Lohan starts bitching and cannot stop, and it all comes out like 'word vomit'. This was a big stage for me. I ran into Adam for the first time since the break-up at a party and it literally ended up in a physical fight. Let's just say years of built-up anger and hurt mixed with alcohol does not work out well.

Staying angry at someone only really affects one person and it's not your ex. Eventually you have to move on to the next stage and GRIEVE for what you have lost. If you were at the point of loving someone, sharing your life with that person, living with them and planning a future with them, then no matter what the anger phase tells you, there must have been some good times. Grieving them will ultimately help set you free.

Now on to the fun stage of a break-up! This is the REBOUND

stage, when you feel confident enough in yourself to get back on the horse and see who else is out there. This is normally when you re-download the dating apps and go out with one intention – to pick up. It is the stage where you get to make up for all the sex you missed out on while you were with your revolting ex. It sounds fun, doesn't it? But, if you're like me, this one can be tricky. At first, I simply felt guilty. I had been with Adam for so long that being with anyone else seemed wrong. Happily, that feeling didn't last.

Moving on, we come to stage nine, LETTING GO. It's that light-bulb moment where you go, *What the fuck was I doing?* This is when you should be focusing on your future rather than your past. This is where I'm at, and I couldn't be happier. Let's not even worry about stage ten. I'm in a good place and I'm just going to skip it.

Now is perhaps a good time to mention that Adam, my cheating ex, has an identical twin brother. His name is Tyler. Tyler is straight and married. I met him on the same day I met Adam at my 21st birthday but obviously I was drawn to the gay brother. Over the years that I was with Adam, I would see Tyler and his wife, Amy, at family events; we'd go to their place for dinner regularly, we'd go out drinking together and see each other at parties all the time. They have become close friends of mine. Even through all the cheating and break-up drama they have remained my friends and ultimately have sided with me as they recognise how much of a bastard Adam has been to me.

I am finally over Adam. I'm not holding onto any hurts

anymore, and can go out for drinks with mutual friends, including Tyler and Amy, without any awkwardness. I mean, I hate the guy but I've just come to the realisation that I deserve better than him and am moving on.

One night a large group of us are out for drinks and a dance. I'm enjoying just letting loose and having a fun night. Towards the end of the night, after way too many drinks, Tyler and Amy approach me on the dance floor. They start dancing on either side of me, both of them rubbing their hands on me. I think it's just fun, don't make anything of it. We move off the dance floor and Tyler whispers into my ear, 'Would you like to come home with us?'

'Yeah sure,' I reply. 'Sharing a taxi makes sense.'

Tyler and Amy look at each other and smile, then Tyler says, 'No, would you like to have a threesome with us?'

I burst out laughing. Either they're joking or I've had too many drinks and didn't hear correctly.

They both stay straight-faced, smile suggestively and tell me they're serious.

I grab Tyler's arm and lead him away from everyone to where I can hear him clearly. I ask him a third time, 'Are you for real?' He says that he and Amy have been talking about it for a while and they're both keen.

But you're the straight brother. You're married. You're Adam's identical twin brother.

All these thoughts race through my head as I struggle to take it in.

But in the end, hey, I don't owe Adam anything.

This could be fun.

The taxi drops us at their house. We go inside to the lounge room and Amy asks if we'd like another drink.

'Yes please!' I reply. I am certainly going to need one.

Amy brings over the drinks and it's a bit uncomfortable and awkward, but we're all so drunk that it doesn't really matter. I'm still not 100 per cent sure that anything will happen.

We sit chatting for a bit and when we finish our drinks, the room goes quiet in anticipation. 'Well, are we doing this?' Amy asks. She gets up, removes her top and bra, and walks towards the bathroom.

Tyler and I make eye contact and one last time I ask, 'Are you sure?'

He smiles and replies, 'Yeah sure, it'll be fun.'

I follow him to the bathroom where Amy's already naked under the shower. Tyler takes his shirt off slowly. He proceeds to unbutton his jeans and steps out of them and into the shower. I immediately notice that his dick is circumcised, a bit of a shock to me as Adam's isn't. I remove my clothes and get in. Amy slides her hands down mine and Tyler's bodies until she has a firm hold of both of our dicks and she starts to kiss me. As we pull away from each other, I make eye contact with Tyler and within seconds I am kissing him. There isn't a lot of room in the shower so we get out, dry off and take it to the bedroom.

As I lie naked in their bed, Tyler on one side of me and Amy on the other, we start kissing each other's bodies and running our hands all over each other. I am really turned on but also a little freaked out, doing things with Tyler who looks so much like Adam – and even more freaked out doing things with any woman, let alone Tyler's wife. I've just spent God knows how long coming to terms with the fact I'm gay and now here I am having sex with a woman. It definitely helps that Tyler's there.

The next morning, we laugh it off as a funny, drunken, one-time thing.

A couple of nights later I go over there for dinner. I pull up to their driveway and head inside, wondering how it'll be.

'Hi,' I say.

'Hey,' Amy replies as Tyler says, 'How ya goin.'

OMG. I can't even make eye contact with them without feeling weird. As I walk further into the house I see Tyler and Amy's girls, who are like nieces to me, and I go over to them and give them a big hug, so that it breaks the ice a little bit. They show me their new scooters as they ride them up and down the hallway.

'We're just having spaghetti bolognese, is that okay?' Amy says from the kitchen.

'Perfect,' I respond and go back to the kids. We play for a while and after Tyler puts them to bed the three of us sit down at the dining table to eat.

It's never been like this before. We make a bit of stilted small talk but mostly it's just the clinking of forks hitting the bottom of bowls, the slurp of spaghetti and the click of glasses of water being placed back on the table.

We finish dinner and move over to the lounge. To my surprise they ask me if I'd like to do it again. This time we're stone cold sober. I look at Tyler and ask him once more if he is okay with it. I'm confused about the roles we all have to play and even more confused about why Adam's straight brother is keen on this. Maybe they're identical inside and out, excluding the penis? But ultimately I'm horny, so I agree and things heat up.

What was supposed to be a one-time thing now becomes a regular thing. In fact, it becomes so frequent that I'm not even hooking up with anyone else. *What in the world is going on?*

And then it dawns on me. I have moved on to stage ten: REVENGE SEX!

I'm not sure how happy I am about that, especially as what was meant to be something fun is now turning into something serious. Conversations are starting to change, feelings are getting involved, and jealousy is kicking in when Amy and Tyler see me talking with other guys, or when my phone dings when I'm around them. Without me even realising it, this 'thing' has turned into somewhat of a relationship – a complicated one – and that is not what I'm looking for.

Things go from bad to worse. Rules are introduced. At first, Amy and Tyler are fine with me hooking up with other people, because that's only fair. They only ask that I tell them about it and that I wear protection. The rules then change. They don't want me hooking up with anyone else. Amy even goes to the extent of completely cock-blocking me when we're out together.

Tyler and Amy come to an agreement between them, which I'm okay with, that they can sleep with me together or individually, which progresses to them coming to my house individually and spending the night.

On the one hand, this is the ultimate revenge, plus I'm getting regular sex on tap with little to no effort at all. I can't stop thinking about all the times Adam cheated on me, all the lies, all the deceit, the multiple STIs, then leaving me for another guy. It gets me off knowing that I'm sleeping with Adam's identical twin brother and his wife, and the fact that it's our secret and Adam has no idea makes it even better. On the flipside, it's a complete mind-fuck. I am so confused. Tyler is practically identical to Adam; he has all the traits I liked about Adam but without the ones I hated. He compliments me and makes me feel good. He has bigger muscles, is smarter, more driven, and, hey, even has a nicer penis than Adam.

Then there's Amy. Firstly, she's a woman for Christ's sake. Also, being with her has given me insight into what a life with a wife and kids could look like, and I am 100 per cent sure that is not what I want. I'd love to be a dad one day, but my ideal co-parent is a man, my true love and soulmate, not a woman. I'm relieved Amy has a Mirena IUD, which is supposed to be a 99 per cent effective contraceptive device. Neither Tyler nor I have been wearing protection because Amy says she is allergic to condoms, but as I'm not really sleeping with anyone else it's not like I can give them anything – and the Mirena takes care of the kid thing.

One day Tyler asks to speak with me. He looks upset and like he hasn't slept in days. He explains that his marriage is falling apart and that he and Amy fight when I'm not around. He says that I make their relationship better. He goes on to tell me Amy doesn't let him touch her unless I'm there. For months now, he continues, she hasn't let him come inside her because she doesn't like it.

Alarm bells go crazy in my head. I reflect on recent conversations with Amy in which she's told me about her sex life with Tyler.

After this talk I decide to cool things as it has become way too involved; also I care about them both too much to be the reason they separate.

Finally, I can breathe. *How did I let this get so messy?* It's beyond me and I regret it, but still want to remain friends and go back to how things used to be.

Easier said than done.

At the beginning of this year I'd left my banking job and started my own mortgage broking business. I'm working out of a corporate office with another broker, my assistant, financial planners and accountants. I have work coming out of my ears and paperwork covering both my desk and the one next to me.

My phone vibrates on the desk, but I can't find it under all the paperwork. I miss the call; it was from Amy. I shoot her a text telling her that I am so busy and will call her later. She replies,

'I really need to talk to you, can you come over now, it is really important, I wouldn't ask unless it was an emergency.' I tell my assistant I have a client appointment and that I'll be back soon.

On the drive over to Amy and Tyler's place, I'm puzzled as to what the emergency is and get nervous she's going to tell me that they have broken up.

I pull up and let myself in through the unlocked front door. Amy's sitting at the dining table with her head in her hands.

'What's happened?' I ask.

She looks up at me and doesn't answer.

I walk over to her and say, 'What's up? What's going on?' She stares at me, stands up and holds up a white piece of plastic. My heart sinks. I'm pretty certain I know what it is but I ask, 'What's that?' I feel like I'm having one of those 'life flashing before your eyes' moments you see in movies.

'I'm pregnant,' she blurts out. 'It's yours, I know it is.'

I am gobsmacked. I step forward, take the pregnancy test from her hand and stare at it. 'What?'

'It can't be Tyler's,' she says, 'he hasn't blown inside me for months.'

I can't fully comprehend this but it matches what Tyler had said to me. I sit down on the lounge in silence. I feel sick to my stomach.

'I'm keeping it, but Tyler doesn't know yet. Can you please help me tell him when he gets home?'

Amy is looking at me. I have so many thoughts running

through my head. *How did I let this go this far? How did this even happen?*

Before I can speak, Amy kneels down in front of me, grabs my hands and says, 'It's going to be okay. I love you and we'll get through this. I don't want to be with Tyler, I want to be with you! Congratulations, you're going to be a dad.'

'Are you crazy?' I snap. Amy stands back up. 'I am not going to be with you, this should never have happened. What are we going to tell people? What is Adam going to say?'

It's suddenly clear to me that Amy is a manipulator. Tyler and I have been pawns in her big life-size game of chess. Did she convince Tyler to have the threesome? Did Amy ever have a Mirena, or did she get it removed without telling us? Was she even allergic to condoms? And then I also wonder, did Tyler use me for sex because he wasn't getting any without me?

What the fuck am I going to do?

What started out as fun has now turned into an unplanned pregnancy. A baby. Why couldn't I have stopped at stage nine of a break-up and just let it go?

I can hear Tyler's van pull up out the front. I want to vomit. Amy and I look at each other, waiting for him to walk in. All I can think is *Why the hell did she choose to tell me before her own husband?*

Tyler walks in the door, sees me and looks confused. Last time I'd spoken to him, I had told him I was backing off and now here I am.

Standing in the doorway, he says, 'What's going on, what are you doing here?'

'Can you tell him?' Amy asks me, putting me on the spot.

'Tell me what?' Tyler replies tightly, looking over at me. I sense he's ready to explode.

'Mate, I'm so sorry,' I say nervously, 'Amy told me it was an emergency and I had to come over. I should have called you before I came round.'

'You're freaking me out, Rod, what the fuck?'

'Amy just told me she's pregnant, man.'

The colour drains from Tyler's face. He looks over at Amy, shaking his head in disbelief.

Before he has a chance to say a word, Amy says, 'No one's to blame here. I don't have a clue whose baby it is and I won't be doing a paternity test until it's born as it can harm the baby.' Her entire tune has changed.

What the? 'Hold on. Just minutes ago you were telling me that you're certain the baby's mine, that you and Tyler hardly ever have sex!'

Tyler jumps in and says, 'Amy! You know as well as I do that if you're actually pregnant then it's definitely Rod's. Come on!'

Amy has been caught in a lie and clearly starts panicking.

'Can't we all just be a family? Why can't you both be the dad? It's 2015, can't we just be a throuple?'

'Are you fucking serious?!' Tyler yells.

I get up from the lounge. I want to be understanding and

supportive as we all got ourselves in to this, but it's just gone too far. 'I am so sorry for getting involved in your marriage – it should never have happened and I will always regret it. I'm going to go so you guys can talk this out. If the baby turns out to be mine, I will love and support it, but I am certainly not doing whatever this is anymore.'

As I leave I can hear Tyler and Amy bickering but I can't be involved anymore. I've caused enough damage.

I'm busy at work a week or so later when my phone dings with a message. It's Adam.

WTF?

'Fuck you, if you wanted to go knock someone up, why the fuck did it have to be my sister-in-law? They're getting a divorce, hope you're happy.'

This news doesn't come as a surprise to me, let's face it. And it does break my heart that I am a huge contributor to this. However, to be attacked by Adam of all people makes me see red.

'This has nothing to do with you Adam and FYI it wasn't just Amy I was sleeping with, it was Tyler too. One thing you should know is that he is better than you in EVERY SINGLE WAY.' With that, I block his number.

Another week passes and I get a call from Amy. I answer with a sinking feeling.

'I'm bleeding,' she cries. 'I think I'm losing the baby.'

'Shit, Amy. Where's Tyler?'

'I don't know' – she's weeping loudly now – 'we've been fighting.'

'Okay, hang on, I'm coming over. I'll take you to the hospital.'

I'm on some kind of autopilot as I leave work, jump in my car and race over to Tyler and Amy's house. When I get there she's still on her own, sobbing. I help her into the car, drive her to the hospital emergency department and guide her in to the triage desk.

But there's plenty of time to think during the long anxious wait together in the emergency room. My emotions get the better of me and I start crying. I am so disappointed and angry with myself. I want to be a dad one day but not like this. And now the baby might be gone.

I walk out to get some air and do the only thing I can think to do in this moment. Call Mum.

'Mum, I'm okay but I'm at the hospital, can you come up to the emergency department?'

'Yes mate,' she says, without hesitation, 'I'm leaving now.'

She gets to the hospital just in time for us to be called to see the doctor. She doesn't judge; she's just there as my support and puts everything else aside in this moment. Even though my mind is a mess, worrying about this baby, I look at Mum with admiration and miss the relationship I once had with her. She stays in the waiting room while we go in.

The doctor asks if I'm the father and Amy jumps in with, 'We don't know.' How embarrassing. The doctor says if we can't be sure then I have to wait outside while they do the ultrasound. I return to Mum in the waiting room.

'Whatever the outcome is, we'll get through this,' she says. 'If there is a baby then it is a beautiful life and you will be a great dad. If the baby is gone, then it's not meant to be, Rod.'

The doctor comes out and tells us that we can go in to Amy. She's crying. 'The baby is gone,' she says.

It's a quiet drive home back to Amy's house. We don't talk at all. I am completely lost for words. Amy won't look in my direction, just stares out the window and cries.

My emotions are all over the place. Part of me is relieved because this was just way too messy to handle but I also feel guilty for being relieved. Another part of me is grieving the loss of the baby, who I'm not 100 per cent was mine.

As we pull up out the front of her house, Amy wipes her tears and pleads with me, 'I know we can be happy together, I just know we can.'

Oh no. 'I can't be with you Amy, I don't feel that way. You know I'm into guys and I should never have let this go so far.'

'Please don't leave me, I can't be alone.'

'Amy, you need to call Tyler to come home to be with you. He's your husband, not me. I can't be with you right now.'

She gets out of the car and I wait for her to go inside. I send Tyler a message telling him he needs to get home to Amy ASAP. Then I drive off, feeling completely lost and so disappointed in myself.

The whole sorry episode creates a lot of confusion for my family. After so many years of fighting with them, trying to convince them I'm gay, now I get myself into a threesome with a married couple and get the wife pregnant. *How proud of me they must be.*

Rather than stress our somewhat-restored yet still fragile relationship, I decide not to explain myself. My parents make sure they are there for me, which is more than enough right now.

What am I supposed to say to them anyway – 'I got so hurt by the person you told me would hurt me that I decided to get revenge and have sex with his twin brother'? They won't understand. The important thing is I know I'm still a gay man. And currently things with my family are okay, on the surface anyway.

12

TIM: Hollywood

Just like Dorothy from *The Wizard of Oz* I've always dreamed of getting swept up in a big gay cyclone full of glitter and being dropped into a world of colour, happiness and acceptance. I've always wanted to be able to skip down the yellow-brick road, hand in hand with other proud gay men, all while wearing my ruby slippers ... okay, thongs so I don't break a leg. The only place I think I can ever experience anything remotely like Dorothy falling into Oz is West Hollywood.

This is the dream that keeps me afloat as I continue the Woolworths Leadership Program in Sydney. Sitting in an office at a desk all day, every day, makes me feel like I'm going insane; I'm a square peg in a round hole. I fantasise about going to America and what life would be like once I eventually moved there.

Then one day I bite the bullet, request my leave and book my flight.

The first time I went to America was in 2000 with my family for a Disneyland trip, and then I returned for a short stay as a bit of a detour on my way home from working in Canada in 2009.

Now that I'm older, wiser and OUT OF THE CLOSET, I want to experience West Hollywood on my own. I feel as though now that I am a proud gay man, I'll be able to delve a lot deeper into what the city has to offer me. I'm going to make this third visit hands-down the best one yet.

Each time I've been there, I've been captivated by Los Angeles, especially the gayest town in the world, West Hollywood. Ever since I returned to Australia, it's been calling my name. I love how full of glitz, glamour and gays West Hollywood is, and seeing as though I have only recently come out to the world, I can't think of a more appropriate place to leap into. To be surrounded not only by like-minded people but also the razzle-dazzle of Hollywood is my absolute dream. I am counting down the days until I can take some time off work and head back to my spiritual home.

On the flight over, I'm bursting with excitement. When I'm not pacing up and down the aisle of the plane, I'm binge-watching Hollywood blockbusters, imagining these superstar actors all having been like me at one point – stuck in a shit job they hated, living a life that didn't fulfil them. As I watch movie after movie, I feel inspired and motivated to do everything in my power to build a life that's much bigger than my current reality. At one point I take my iPod into the bathroom and lock the door. I start to blast music in my ears and dance around, lip-syncing to the bathroom mirror.

Let me paint a picture for you of West Hollywood. First of all, 99.9 per cent of the population is gay, so basically being straight here makes you the minority. Rainbow flags stretch as far as the eye can see all the way down glorious Sunset Strip. At night the streets throb with gay nightlife and throughout the day the sidewalks overflow with gay guys strutting to the gym, grabbing iced coffees and chatting about Ariana Grande's new album.

Cries of 'Yassssssss', 'Okurrrrrrr' and 'You Better Werk Bitch' echo through the city, every second shop is painted pink, and it seems like even the homeless people have been dressed by a fabulous gay stylist. Everything is colourful, everything is glamorous, and everything is exactly what I wish my life Down Under looked like.

West Hollywood is like the Gay Neverland I used to dream of flying away to as a kid and I want to be a part of it forever. I love the buzz of celebrity sightings, the pop culture landmarks on every corner, the over-the-top fashion. I love being surrounded by people like me who are all proud and comfortable in their own skin.

I love all the sequin-covered, sparkly distraction from all the struggles I face back home. I'm still drinking probably more than I should be, still exercising like crazy and have big issues with my body and food, but here it doesn't control every second of my entire day. I want this feeling of liberation to last for as long as possible and as I'm walking down Santa Monica Boulevard, I look up at the Hollywood sign and make a promise to myself:

After this holiday, I am going to do everything in my power to come back and live and work here.

I bump into some really nice, fun new people at a café in West Hollywood and tell them I am fresh off the plane from Australia. We get chatting and they decide to take me on a private tour around Hollywood. It sounds super sketchy, but they are all so nice and I am caught up in the moment and think, *Why not*. We all jump in the car, blast Ariana Grande's new album and begin the tour. We drive down Hollywood Boulevard with the wind in our hair, waving at the hundreds of tourists that scatter the iconic 'Walk of Fame' sidewalk. We make our way through Beverly Hills, past mega mansions of the rich and famous, passing the Playboy Mansion, the infamous Beverly Hills Hotel and even Christina Aguilera's house. Our final stop is the Hollywood Hills. As the music blasts we weave our way through the hills. This picturesque hillside neighbourhood had the best views in LA and overlooked the city, an endless hazy mirage I know is filled with opportunity and success. The millions of people in the city below are all just like me, I think, chasing their dreams in the city of fame, excess and fortune. As I gaze over the hill side below, I freeze in amazement. The huge iconic Hollywood sign is directly below us on the hillside, literally just metres away, its huge white letters towering over the city like a never-ending reminder to never give up on your dreams. As I breathe in deeply, I make a promise to myself that I will make that scared and afraid outcast loser from my past proud.

At night West Hollywood comes alive with a sea of rainbow lights, confetti and every gay anthem known to humankind. Men scurry up and down the main stretch, visiting the many iconic gay clubs and partying the night away. I've never been to a gay night club before and I'm happy that my first time will be at one of West Hollywood's famous clubs, The Abbey. As I make my way down the street my senses are in overdrive. Huge billboards featuring the world's biggest celebrities grace every corner, while the hundreds of clubs, restaurants and hotels lining the street are almost as famous as the celebrities who frequent them. I am lost in a dancing kaleidoscope of colours and I can't wait to see what the night brings.

Everyone waiting in line is already in the party spirit and dancing with each other as the music floods the main street. The energy is infectious, and I'm getting more and more excited and then I see the huge and black metal gates of this iconic club. I feel so lucky and privileged to be here.

As I enter the night club I am immediately filled with adrenaline.

There are go-go dancers twerking like Energiser Bunnies on multiple platforms throughout the club. These ripped, muscly men have huge penises bulging through their tiny lace jockstraps. They dance around the entire club, hanging from the rafters in the ceiling then effortlessly landing on the bar doing the splits. The muscular, oiled-up bar staff all in skimpy black tank tops look like something out of a gay stripper convention. Some of the bar staff are even serving drinks shirtless and the majority of men waiting for their turn are practically salivating. The dance floor's packed with half-naked men grinding and rubbing on each other like it's the last night of their lives. The private VIP booths are filled with gay couples making out and grabbing each other's arses. The dark-wood interior gives it a very medieval vibe, like I've stepped into the gay version of *Game of Thrones*.

This place is incredible. People are completely letting go and dancing as freely as their hearts desire. No one looks like they care at all about how outrageous their dance moves may seem. This is a dream come true. Boys are dancing with boys, boys are kissing boys and there are even male dancers up on the bar doing a full-blown dance routine like something out of *Coyote Ugly*.

As I start dancing, I'm approached by a group of locals on a night out. Somehow, over the blasting music, we spark up a conversation and they're immediately intrigued by my broad Aussie accent. They compliment me on my voice, my clothes, the way I look. I can't believe this group of sexy men is showering me with affection. The drinks flow and the flirtation increases. I've only ever experienced validation like this from Instagram but now it's physical, face to face and from multiple, real men. The initial subtle gestures turn into straight-up booty slaps and bulge grabs. I can feel myself gravitating towards the tallest one, lean, chiselled and handsome.

'Hi, what's your name?' I ask.

'John,' he replies. He has a dreamy American accent.

John towers over us all on the dance floor. I make eyes at him and he pulls me close, and we begin kissing in front of everyone in the mass of intertwined dancing bodies.

After what feels like hours of dancing and kissing John, he asks if I want to go home with him. I am so turned on. 'A hundred per cent let's do it!' I yell.

Then he leans in and murmurs in my ear, 'Do you mind if a good friend comes back to my house for a few more drinks with us?'

Sounds fun to me. 'No worries,' I say.

The three of us jump in an Uber and head back to John's apartment in Beverly Hills. As we fly through the streets, I feel like one of the Real Housewives of Beverly Hills being driven by her private chauffeur on the way to her luxury home. When we pull up at John's fancy apartment and jump out, I can't believe where I am. In the moonlight I can make out the iconic rows of palm trees lining a street full of huge mansions. These are the homes of the rich and famous and in this moment, I feel like a real Hollywood celebrity. The thousands of bright stars in the night sky look like millions of cameras flashing all at once, as if I'm surrounded by a crowd of paparazzi. I am in Hollywood Heaven.

John gives me a tour of his gorgeous pad, the perfect balance between modern architecture and classical details. A huge chandelier in the dining room looks brighter than the starry night outside. Everything has glamourous finishes. A large infinity pool out the back is lit up with turquoise-coloured lights and there's a tiny little dressed-up dog that looks like it might have been stolen straight from Paris Hilton's mansion up the street.

Back inside, John leads us straight to his bedroom and offers us drinks. By this point I'm very drunk yet incredibly horny. Suddenly John's friend leans in and begins touching John's leg. The leg touching slowly leads to them taking each other's shirts off and eventually they start kissing in front of me.

'What's going on here?' I blurt out while they have their tongues down each other's throats. I thought they were just friends, and that John was only interested in doing things with me.

John looks me in the eye and says, 'We're just friends but when we drink, we get together. Do you want to join us?'

Woah. I've only ever been with one guy before, never two. Do they just want to do a three-way kiss or have a full-blown threesome? I've seen gay threesomes in pornos before but I certainly don't know what to do or where to go. I'm really attracted to John, though, and his friend is good-looking.

I nod. I've felt so liberated all night long so why stop now?

With that, we tear each other's clothes off and soon the three of us are rolling around on John's bed, kissing and touching every part of each other's bodies.

I'm kissing the friend when John bends me over and starts to slide inside me. This is only the second time I've done anal. The first time it felt romantic and I enjoyed every second of it.

But John is a lot more well-endowed than the guy I lost my butt virginity to, so this is not a very pleasant experience. The combination of John's monstrous cock and basically no foreplay makes me moan in pain, not pleasure. What's worse is there's not just one person witnessing my pathetic attempt at taking a huge penis but two. I try hard to look like I'm enjoying it but can't help squirming uncomfortably and burying my face in the pillow.

Then a disgusting, potent smell hits me. *OMG! Every gay man's worst nightmare is happening to me right now!* I immediately jump up and run to the bathroom, hop in the shower and wash myself off. *I have just made a total fool of myself in front of these two hot dudes.*

I'm drying myself off when John walks in. 'It's happened to all of us at one point or another so don't stress,' he says. 'Did you douche before you came out tonight?'

'What the hell is that?' I ask.

'Ah. Most of the time when guys have sex, they douche beforehand.' I look at him blankly. 'Like, you rinse out and clean your ass before anal sex.' Now I'm even more embarrassed. I'd had no idea.

As humiliating as the night is, John and his friend reassure me about it, which makes me feel a bit better. And on the bright side, I've learned what to do so it never happens again. First thing next morning, I run down to the main shops in West Hollywood and buy the first douche I can find.

I realise there's a lot of things about gay culture I'm oblivious to. There are many things I still need to learn, but that excites me, and I'm determined to become the best gay version of myself.

Before I know it, my two weeks are up. I don't want to leave America. West Hollywood has been the most liberating time of my life. It has been a crazy, fun-filled adventure and I wish it could last forever. I'm not ready to return to being in the minority and mundane again. The thought of going back to a city where I know zero gay people is torture.

Sitting on the plane as it speeds down the LAX runway, my heart aches with sadness. But as much as I don't want to leave, I'm getting low on money and hey, a holiday can't last forever.

As the plane takes off, I make out the Hollywood sign in the distance, towering over the city, a reminder to do whatever it takes to accomplish the American Dream. For me, the famous sign has become symbolic of the dream life I crave so desperately. I watch it disappear, Miley Cyrus's 'Party in the USA' blasting through my headphones, and repeat my vow to return one day and let nothing stand in my way.

13

ROD: My Aussie bogan Prince Charming

Despite everything they've said and done, I still have this longing to please my parents. I come up with a new plan to try to win their acceptance while staying true to who I am. I dream that if I bring a Christian boy home then they might accept him … and me.

My plan gets a boost sooner than I expect. I've just started seeing this guy, Jackson, I met on a dating app. We're getting along really well and then I notice his screensaver: 'I can do all things through Christ who gives me strength.' I recognise it immediately. I even know that it's Philippians 4:13.

'Is that a Bible verse on your phone?' I blurt out. He turns his phone over, embarrassed. I reassure him that it's okay and start telling him that I come from a Christian home and have attended church for years, which starts a long conversation about 'Being Gay' and 'Being a Christian'. He tells me how involved he is in music and he evens sings at his church.

As I sit there listening to Jackson I see so much of myself in him; I can feel his pain. I know exactly what he's going through except that while I've been dealing with this for the best part of a decade, Jackson's thirty and still has not come to terms with who he is. I want to help him.

We start seeing more of each other. It's great through the week; he seems confident in himself and makes me feel good. He is shaping up to be boyfriend material. And then the weekend rolls around. He gets up and takes himself to church, where he puts on a front as a good Christian boy, and all I can think is he better be repenting for what we got up to before he left my bed. He comes back over after church and is conflicted and feeling sorry for himself. He tells me that he still thinks that God can heal him of his attraction to men. This hits a nerve. The torture of hoping and then being dashed down over and over again has made me want to kill myself in the past and I don't want him to go through what I did.

When I help Jackson move to a new house, I get to meet his parents. He says, 'Mum and Dad, this is my friend Rod, he's helping me move.' It's all so familiar.

I've cut back on drinking and partying for Jackson but he still thinks I have a drinking problem … because his only other friends are from his church and think it's a sin to get drunk. This is mainly because I got drunk at my birthday party and at New Year's, two days most people get smashed. He should have seen me before we met!

If I'm honest with myself, I'm not even really attracted to him, not in the way you should be attracted to someone you want to be with. I just want to be able to introduce him to my parents.

I want him to realise there's not anything wrong with him being gay. Meanwhile, I'm getting the opposite message from him. I've been told by so many people in my life that 'gay is wrong', I really don't need it from a boyfriend.

I give all this a lot of thought but before I can bring myself to do anything about it, Jackson tells me he wants to talk. He dumps me to 'focus on God'. Worse, he then realises he wants me back, has sex with me, stays the night and ends it again in the morning. The last thing he sees of me is my door slamming in his face.

So much for boyfriend material.

I move on from Jackson to an older guy who turns out to be only using me to make his best friend jealous, and then to a guy who has just been in gaol ... as in, we start seeing each other the week he's released! He's actually an incredibly nice guy; he's just been caught up with the wrong people and made mistakes. But ultimately he's not for me. Maybe after Jackson the closeted Christian I just needed something 'naughty'.

I'm really starting to question whether I'll meet someone who gets me. *I'm going to be that lonely old rich guy who looks like the out-of-place sleaze in a club trying to get some.*

Gradually, I give up on the whole concept of a future with a guy. It's easier to be alone.

One day I'm scrolling through Grindr hoping for the heading 'Visiting' or for a new profile to pop up. Usually it's the same profiles every single day and I get messages saying 'Hey' or 'Hi' and nothing else. Then when I don't reply they just type the word again ten times over. Sometimes they don't take the hint and proceed to send nudes. *Wow, thank you faceless profile, I will definitely have sex with you now.*

If it's not this, it's the closeted married men with kids looking for some fun on the side, or on rare occasion a catfish – a good-looking guy who talks to me for days on end and turns out to be a fake profile – or a guy who simply starts a conversation and then disappears for days at a time.

Today I spot a profile for a guy named Tim that Cupid might have described as 'hot as fuck'. He is the first sexy-as-hell dude I've seen on this app so I start a conversation. He tells me I'm hot and we chat for a bit. Based on his shirtless profile pic, I assume he's a player, but I don't care. I'm more than happy to be played by him. The conversation flows, but then simply stops. This happens a few times, sometimes for a week, and then he reappears. I'm certain he's a catfish or fake profile. After weeks of seeing his profile disappear and reappear multiple times, I lose interest.

That is until one day a good friend of mine sends me a link to a Facebook profile with a message saying, 'Check this guy out, he's single and you two would be perfect together.' I click on the link and to my surprise it's Tim, the fake profile. I ignore it.

Then later that day, I receive a friend request from Tim. Now I'm intrigued. I accept the request and soon afterwards a message arrives. 'Hi mate, how are ya?' he writes. He goes on to ask the same questions he did on Grindr and I immediately lose interest again. Definitely a catfish.

But this time Tim keeps up the conversation. He asks me lots of questions about myself, is very cute and full-on with the compliments, which I'm not complaining about. It doesn't take him long to ask me out on a date. The new *Pirates of the Caribbean* movie is out, and Tim is hanging to see it.

The first time he asks, I have 'plans'.

He asks me a second time; I have a 'headache'.

The third time I'm tired from work. Who knows why but he asks a fourth time, and I say, 'Look, how about you just come over and we can watch a movie at my place?' Good ol' Netflix and chill. He is keen and we make a date.

On the day Tim's coming over, I'm still thinking, *Is this guy real?* I'm a bit self-conscious because of how gorgeous he looks in his photos. I have butterflies in my stomach. I don't get nervous about meeting guys; this is new to me.

I clear any work appointments I have that afternoon so I can get home to clean the house. I make it spotless. I then have the longest shower of my life. I wash and rewash one hundred times. I wash the hair on my head and manscape everything else, so I am looking fine. I get out of the shower and put on practically an entire can of deodorant and cover myself from head to toe in cologne. He'll be able to smell me from down the street.

Why am I freaking out?

My phone dings and it's a message from Tim. 'I'm out the front,' it reads. I tell him to come up to the house. My chest is thumping. I have a minute to apply even more deodorant and give myself another hundred spritzes of cologne. There's a knock on the door, and I open it.

He is even better-looking than his photos.

'Hey mate, how are ya? I'm Tim,' he says. His smile melts me; he has the pearliest white, straight teeth. His deep masculine voice is so sexy I want to rip his clothes off then and there. He looks at me with his beautiful blue eyes like he is staring into my soul. He's wearing denim shorts and a loose-fitting singlet showing off a little side boob. I think I have found my Aussie bogan Prince Charming, without the beer gut and thongs. Actually, he does have thongs on.

Get it together, Rod. I shake his hand and say, 'Come on in.'

Tim might be nervous too because he will not shut up. He's really interested in me and wants to know everything. He's giggly and so gorgeous. After we have a drink downstairs, I ask if he wants to go up and watch a movie. We grab another bevvie and proceed upstairs, Tim still talking all the way. We lie down on the bed next to each other; I move my hand to Tim's leg and softly rub up and down in a suggestive way. This is the first time Tim has stopped talking since he arrived. He gazes down at my hand, then straight into my eyes. I lean in, place my hand on the back of Tim's head and kiss him.

FIREWORKS. This feels like an out-of-body experience.

I have never experienced anything like this before. Every care in the world vanishes, I feel safe and secure. I feel whole.

It's the most passionate, amazing night of my life. The soul connection we feel with each other is amazing. *What have I been missing out on my whole life?* I had been in a relationship for years, had one-night stands and little flings along my journey, but this is something else, and I am not letting it go in a hurry.

After Tim leaves, I run into my housemate Bec's room in excitement and tell her, 'I think I just met my husband.'

She replies, 'I heard.'

We begin dating. First we see the *Pirates* movie Tim has been begging me to go to. It's a late session on a Saturday night so we decide to make it a full Date Night. The movies are in a big shopping complex with an outdoor plaza area that has restaurants and bars. Seems like everyone has the same idea as there's a buzzing crowd.

As we walk out into the plaza, I naturally grab hold of Tim's hand and we head to a bar to have a drink or two before the movie. As we walk, I notice that Tim has the biggest smile on his face, but I think he may also be a little nervous as he keeps rubbing his thumb up and down my hand. We're getting a few looks from people, as gay people aren't common in Newcastle.

We walk into the bar, the lights are dimmed and there's a guy playing acoustic guitar in the corner. We grab a high round table with a couple of stools next to this huge artwork of Britney Spears performing (fate, right?), and Tim offers to get the first round of drinks. My eyes follow him to the bar. He's wearing light-blue skinny jeans that make his butt look so damn cute. He looks over his shoulder and smiles broadly; he knows I'm checking him out. Tim orders our vodka, lime and sodas with straws, picks them up and starts walking back. I feel like everything has been slowed down for dramatic effect as this godlike man walks towards me.

Tim sits down and we're both grinning non-stop. I reach over and grab Tim's hand on top of the table, and it feels so right to me. People are walking by in this busy bar yet there's not one part of me that feels embarrassed.

Tim looks over at me and says, 'Can I tell you something?'

'Yeah of course.'

'I've never done this before.'

'What, been on a date?' I ask.

'No, held a dude's hand in public.'

If I wasn't melting already I am about to be a puddle of love on the floor. Those words make me feel so safe and secure and all my worries and reservations about getting into something serious with Tim fly out the window.

After the movie, we go back to my house, put on some music, light a few candles and jump in the shower together. This is shaping up to be the best date night ever. As we're talking and rubbing soap all over each other, a song comes on. It's Ariana Grande's version of 'Beauty and the Beast'. As it plays, I look up at Tim and see tears in his eyes. He puts his arms around me and kisses me. He then proceeds to rest his head on my shoulder and starts swaying side to side. Yes, we are slow dancing in the shower. I know in this moment that I am falling in love with Tim and I feel in my heart that he loves me back.

Tim pulls away, his blue eyes intense. Then he leans in and gives me a slow, passionate kiss with the most perfect amount of tongue. I'm floating.

We turn the water off, step out of the shower and grab our towels. Tim stands there drying his hair. I'm mesmerised by the water dripping down his chest and abs ... I feel like I'm watching real-life porn in slo-mo. My eyes follow the water down to his groin, where I notice how hard his dick is, which makes me so turned on I'm practically trembling. Still dripping wet, I step in close and our erections touch. I take his face in my hands and begin kissing him again. My lips travel around to his neck and I bite him ever so softly, then move up to his ear lobe and begin sucking on it. I hear Tim's sharp intake of breath; the sounds he makes are sending me crazy. I grab his ass with both hands and lift him up as he wraps his legs around me, then carry him over to the bed and lay him down. I kiss his neck again, slowly making my way down his muscular body. As I get to his nipples, I give them a lick and a little bite. Tim groans like he's about to come but I don't want it to end just yet, so I head further to his abs, licking his 'V' all the way down to his groin and tease his balls. I kiss him down one thigh and back up the other until I reach his now enormous dick. I take hold of it and begin slowly sucking as Tim's moans of pleasure get even louder.

Kissing back up his body, I reach over to the bedside table, and grab the lube from the drawer. I look deep into Tim's eyes as he smirks up at me and wraps his legs around my body. I lean down and kiss him passionately as I enter him. 'Just go nice and slow,' he whispers to me. *Why has sex never felt like this?* It's like I'm a part of Tim and the connection is indescribable. With every thrust, it feels like we're falling more and more in love and completely giving ourselves to each other. We come at the same time and for me it's the longest, most intense orgasm of my life.

The next day, we are inseparable and spend the day at the beach together. We pack the bluetooth speaker, a couple of towels, a cooler with a four-pack of Tim's sugar-free Smirnoff double blacks and the beach umbrella. Dudley Beach is very quiet and unpatrolled and we have it practically to ourselves.

We put up our umbrella and turn the music on, playing all of our favourite pop princesses – which turn out to be the same. In no time our hands are all over each as we make out under the shade of our umbrella. We're like love-struck teenagers. Katy Perry's 'Girls Just Wanna Have Fun' with Nicki Minaj comes on and Tim jumps to his feet and starts singing at the top of his lungs and dancing around – this is after only one drink, by the way. He is shaking his cute little butt in his speedos. He grabs my hand, pulls me to my feet and my inner popstar comes to the surface. Next minute we're bumping and grinding, waving our arms around like complete idiots and laughing uncontrollably.

I can't remember the last time someone has made me laugh-cry this hard, if ever.

At the end of our beach day we pack up our things and head home, and I promise Tim I'll cook up my famous spaghetti bolognese. Back in the kitchen, cooking is tricky as I have a glass of red in one hand, a wooden spoon in the other while Tim stands behind me, kissing my neck. He cannot keep his hands off me.

We have a lovely candlelit dinner, so at ease and so happy.

'Did you like it?' I ask.

'It was delicious, mate, thank you,' he says. Tim always calls me 'mate', which at first I hate. *I'm not just your mate, mate.*

He lets out a little laugh.

'You didn't like it?' I start laughing too.

'I don't really eat red meat,' he says, 'or pasta!' and cracks up completely.

'Whhhhaaaat, why didn't you tell me?' I say, feeling embarrassed but still laughing.

'I just want to make you happy. I'll eat anything you make for me,' he says.

Part of me can't help being amused but another part is horrified. I didn't even ask if he eats red meat! I jump up, run around and give him the biggest hug, telling him, 'I'm so sorry, can I cook you something else?'

Tim just looks up at me and says, 'Honestly, it was delicious. I just don't normally eat this.' We both cannot stop laughing, and I look back at him and think, *This guy is perfect.* My heart is melting. He is everything I've ever dreamed of: he's smart, sexy, kind, rocks my world in the bedroom and will do anything to make me happy. What a catch.

Everything is perfect except for one thing. Tim might be leaving. He's studying for a personal training certificate and when he finishes he plans to fulfil his lifelong dream of going to live in LA. He is upfront about this from the start and I try to guard my heart and protect myself from being hurt. While we're only a new thing, it's stronger than anything I've ever felt before.

One afternoon we go to a local beach headland to watch the sunset. We can see up and down the coastline for kilometres. The sun's going down and there's not a breath of wind. The ocean looks like glass with a beautiful orange and pink tinge.

Tim and I cuddle up next to each other.

I'm starting to feel a bit uneasy about how strong my feelings for him are. I don't doubt how he feels, but I don't want to be the one who gets in the way of something he wants to do so badly. The sun disappears and we share a beautiful romantic kiss.

We head back to the car and I drive us over to my place. I park the car in the garage but don't get out.

'Tim, can I talk to you about something?'

'Yeah mate, of course.'

I'm nervous about bringing up America in case Tim decides to end things now, but I have to get it off my chest.

'I am honestly so happy right now and you know I'm not seeing anyone else,' I say, 'but I'm really afraid that I'm going to get hurt.'

'Who knows what the future may bring,' says Tim, as he leans forward and puts his hand on my leg. 'All I know is I want to be with you.'

'Does that mean you're my boyfriend now?' I say and giggle.

'Of course I'm your boyfriend, I've thought of myself as your boyfriend since the day we met, mate,' he says. 'Let's live for today.'

We both hate winter, so a month into our relationship we book a trip to Bali. Tickets bought, I decide to let my parents know that I've met someone and we're going on holiday together. I want to avoid another fight and more heartache so I decide to call Mum rather than visit.

'I don't want to fight or cause drama, Mum,' I say, getting straight to the point. 'I know how you feel about me being gay but out of respect for you and Dad, I'm letting you know that I'm seeing someone and he makes me really happy.'

There's a pause. I'm glad we're on the phone so I don't have to see Mum's face.

'You're right, you do know how we feel about it and you know we don't agree with it,' she says.

'Look Mum, like I said, how you feel doesn't change the fact

I'm with someone but I don't want things to turn out the way they did when I was with Adam.'

'Neither do we, Rod,' she says.

'We're off to Bali next week and I thought you should know.'

'Thanks for telling me,' she says, and we end the call.

That went better than I thought it would, I think to myself.

The phone rings straightaway and it's Dad.

'Look mate, your mum just told me that you have some new fella and you're going to Bali or something,' he says.

'Yes Dad, like I said to Mum, I don't want to fight over it. There's nothing you can do about it and I'm just letting you know,' I say confidently, although I'm beginning to feel sick.

'You know our family is private so all I ask is that you keep your gay bullshit off Facebook,' he says.

Gay bullshit. Unbelievable. 'Dad, are you kidding?!' I yell. 'You would never ask Kelly, Matt or Emma not to put their holiday photos up on Facebook, so why would you ask me?'

'Just respect what I'm telling you, mate, it's not right.'

I end the call, pull up Facebook and post my first photo with Tim with a caption that reads, 'This time next week I will be flying out to Bali with this stud' as a huge middle finger to my dad.

Bali is the most romantic holiday imaginable, sunbaking in our private pool villa in Seminyak, drinking cocktails. I even arrange rose petals to fill the pool and the bath, and we have a private poolside dinner and champagne. It is picture perfect, all of which I post on Facebook like anyone would. Naturally I want to keep those memories but I also go above and beyond because Dad told me not to.

One night we decide to go clubbing. In the Tim and Rod style we've already established, we hit the town hard. We start with some drinks at the villa and warm up with a Beyoncé megamix. We're already buzzing by the time we head out. After some margarita jugs and a mariachi band at the famous Mexicola restaurant, we head to Mixwell, a well-known gay club among our friends. After a bucket of vodka and Red Bull we hit the dance floor. At one point we head to the toilets and get lost on the way back. We see a set of stairs and are curious to see where they lead and then we stumble upon a bunch of drag queens and go-go dancers getting ready for a performance.

I run over to the dancers who are wearing nothing but tight gold speedos and chains and I beg them for us to be in the show. With no hesitation they hand me two outfits. Tim is over with the drag queens talking up a storm when I tap him on the shoulder and give him his speedos.

'Put these on, we're in the show,' I tell him. Most people would be like 'no way I am not wearing that', but not Tim.

'Fuck yeah!' he says, grabs the gear and is changed in a second.

We're all making our way down the stairs when Tim and I say we have no idea about the choreography.

'Just dance and have fun,' they say.

And that's what we do. I think listening to Beyoncé prior to going out actually makes us think we're her because we steal the show.

Back on the dance floor later, I look at Tim and think, *I can be myself and nothing but myself around him – he is so much like me.* I'm so happy I can hardly contain it and I yell, 'I LOVE YOU!'

Tim immediately gives me one of his sexy little smirks and says, 'I LOVE YOU TOO, MATE!' The next morning we tell each other again, just to make sure it wasn't the booze.

We fly home to Australia on cloud nine, head over heels in love with each other.

I drive Tim back to his mum's house then go home to unpack. I'm chatting excitedly to Bec about the trip when the phone rings. It's Dad. *Here we go.*

'Hi, Dad,' I say.

'Mate, I am not happy. I told you to have some respect for us and not put your gay bullshit all over the internet for the world to see!'

'My gay bullshit? They were holiday photos with my partner. You seem to be the only one who doesn't like them! Everyone else on Facebook is commenting how beautiful the pics are and you're here yelling at me!'

'I asked you to do one thing and you threw it in our faces. It's just not right mate, it's disgusting,' he tells me. *That hurts.*

Bec looks at me in disbelief. I take a deep breath and yell down the phone, 'You know what, Dad? If you and the family can't accept me for me, and love me for me, then maybe we should just go our separate ways!'

'Fine, if that's what you want mate, *fine*,' Dad replies.

'I don't even know who you are anymore, you're certainly not my dad,' I tell him and hang up.

I collapse to the floor and let out the most painful cry. Bec hugs me. 'I'm your family, you have so many people who love you,' she says as she cries with me on the floor.

Bec picks up my phone and calls Tim, and he rushes back over to be by my side. When he arrives I tell him.

'I don't have family anymore.'

14

TIM: The American Dream

To put it bluntly, Newcastle wasn't exactly overflowing with eligible gay bachelors when Rod and I met. In fact it seemed to be in the middle of a record-breaking dry spell. The few Grindr guys I did hook up with or even just chatted to in Newie just didn't tick the boxes for me that I so desperately wanted ticked.

It felt like it was impossible for me to meet someone like me and no matter how many random Grindr chats I started, there was never any chemistry. This sounds ridiculous because in the gay world Grindr is a very stereotypical dating app used mainly for hook-ups, but I craved something more meaningful and longer lasting than just a booty call. Most guys I chatted to on Grindr either wanted meaningless sex, or were eager for me to be the third in their gay open relationship, or faceless profiles who are clearly married straight men living a secret double life or catfish profiles.

I just wanted to find someone who felt like my best mate, who was sexy, charming, genuine and fun. I just wanted a sexy Prince Charming who was into dudes. Was that too much to ask?

Every time I downloaded Grindr, I'd only use it for a few days then delete it out of frustration. I was also living in between Mum's and Dad's houses, forty-five minutes from each other. Every time I went to Dad's in Port Stephens, I dropped out of Newcastle on Grindr, making *me* look like a catfish.

I also had huge reservations that if I did happen to meet someone I really liked, I didn't want them to stand in the way of my American dream. So on one hand I wanted to meet my gay best mate but at the same time didn't want to meet someone amazing because it could flip my life plan entirely on its head.

However, as much as I resisted, destiny had a different idea. I stumbled across Rod's Grindr profile and we hit it off straightaway. After a few weeks of chatting on the app we decided to meet up for our first date. *OMG!*

As I pull up to Rod's place for the very first time, I am so incredibly nervous. I think this is going to be another let-down like every other Grindr date. But Rod seems to be a stand-up guy, his photos are sexy and the chats we have are fun and easy.

I take a deep breath. *Fuck it, let's do this!* I get out of the car, walk up to Rod's door and knock. I literally have my fingers crossed.

What happens next is incredible, a cross between the opening of a gay Disney movie and the greatest gay porn film. The door flings open and standing in front of me is a tall, sexy man with the hottest sleeve tattoo I've ever seen. He's wearing a singlet that shows off his tanned, bulging biceps and has perfectly shaped designer stubble that frames his model-like face. He has seduction in his eyes. I reach out to shake his hand and am greeted with a very firm handshake. That's enough to make me go weak at the knees. You can cut the sexual tension with a knife. I sense in that moment we want to rip each other's clothes off and have the raunchiest sex of our lives.

Instead we both stand in the doorway making cute but clearly nervous conversation. I don't want to jump the gun, but it already feels like everything I want in a guy is standing directly in front of me. He's super sexy, seems incredibly genuine and is so easy to talk too. Too good to be true, right? Is this dude a drug dealer on the run or some lunatic who's about to hold me captive in his sex dungeon?

There's no way this guy could be so perfect and live literally a few minutes from my childhood home, I think as I fall deeper into the handsome stud energy Rod's exuding. I remain hopeful as we walk inside and he closes the door behind me.

We later go on our first real date night in a social setting. This is a ground-breaking moment for me: while I've obviously done things with men before, it's the first time in my life I openly show public displays of affection with another man.

We go to a bar at the shopping centre near where we both live. As we arrive, I'm excited to spend the next few hours getting to know each other even better. While we're walking through the shopping centre to the bar, Rod grabs my hand and squeezes it tight. I glance over to him, and he has a huge proud smile plastered across his face. We're now walking hand in hand past mums, dads, children and grandparents all looking at us. Some people even seem to have a shocked or confused look on their faces.

I hesitate and for a split second, feel myself question what we're doing. *Will people think we're weird and laugh at us?* I immediately replace this self-doubt with an overwhelming sense of pride. I've spent so many years lying to the world about who I truly am and now I'm walking hand in hand with the man I have the hots for so bad, so openly in public.

It's as if Rod's passing his contagious, electric feeling of pride through his palm and into my body. This addictive feeling of self-love and happiness flows through every part of me and I begin to feel like a superhero. I'm like the gay version of Superman, with my big red cape blowing in the wind as I'm strutting along. Out of pure excitement I can feel myself grasping Rod's hand tighter and tighter with each step. I think back to my younger self who would never have had the courage to show his truth to the world. I feel like I'm making my childhood self proud in this moment. A beaming smile bursts across my nervous expression.

As we arrive at the bar Rod pulls me in tight and we lock eyes. In this beautiful loving moment, I want to kiss him so bad, but I've never done this before with what feels like a huge crowd watching on and glaring at us. I am nervous and want to kiss the man of my dreams so bad but I'm worried we'll cause a scene. I can feel my love for Rod flowing through every vein in my body and I want to scream it from the rooftops, but I'm second-guessing myself.

As I look deeply into Rod's eyes I can't control it any longer. I'm proud of myself, I'm proud of Rod and most of all I'm proud of what we represent together: change. This is all that matters and as we lock lips it feels like the world stops around us.

Even though I feel everyone watching on with confusion and disbelief, my heart is so happy and I want this moment to last forever. Also, in the back of my mind I hope there will be a confused boy just like my childhood self who will see two men kissing and it makes him feel hope and not so alone and frightened.

We go into the bar and start having a few drinks together. This is also the first time I've been in a public place with a guy I have feelings for, showing him affection. Rod caresses my leg and showers me with compliment after compliment. He is kissing me on the cheek every few minutes and slaps my butt every time I get up from the table and walk to the bar. This is everything I had dreamed about as a little gay boy – feeling free to be in public with my best mate who I love so deeply and showcase our love to the world.

When you find your soulmate who truly gets you, it is a phenomenal feeling. I'm no longer scared and afraid to be myself and am always encouraged by Rod to 'never let anyone dull your sparkle'. Dancing around the house in crazy wigs, singing our hearts out to Beyoncé in the shower and dressing up in ridiculous outfits and doing runway fashion shows together sounds silly but it is a daily occurrence for us and what I have always craved. With Rod, I don't have to pretend that my favourite colour isn't pink, or my favourite singer is not Britney Spears. I don't have to hide the fact I love the Kardashians or am worried to ask him to fake tan my back. I'm not concerned he will judge me for wearing women's fragrances and am not afraid he will shame me for knowing every single word to the Celine Dion song in *Titanic*, 'My Heart Will Go On'. We are two gay peas in a pod, and to be loved by someone who encourages my outrageous and random quirks is everything I had ever been searching for in a partner.

'OMG we're running late!' Rod screams. We're flying down the highway with the wind blowing our hair and Rihanna blaring from the radio. Today is the day Rod has been talking about nonstop for weeks: we're on our way to look at a litter of German shepherd puppies. Sounds cute, right? No, this is my worst nightmare. Ever since the day I met Rod he has talked about his dream to own a German shepherd.

I was horrified by the thought. This was the complete opposite pet to what I'd always imagined myself getting when I was older. Growing up, my dream dog was a tiny little chihuahua that I could dress up in fairy costumes and carry around in a handbag. I wanted a teacup dog that I would call Tinkerbell, take her with me everywhere, and even have a life-size Barbie doghouse for her to call home. I was desperate to live out my Paris Hilton fantasy, and a huge ugly German shepherd wasn't going to cut it. But this is Rod's dream and I am so deeply in love with him that I just want him to be happy.

'Are you excited to meet our little boy?' Rod asks, smiling from ear to ear. Up until this point I'd just been totally agreeing with everything he said about it, not thinking it would ever become a reality.

Ignoring his question, I say, 'Where the fuck are we?' We're pulling into a property that looks more like the set of *Wolf Creek* than a dog breeders. What I see next is like a horror scene: two huge German shepherd beasts galloping around a large paddock, wrestling each other. They're covered in mud with a thick stream of drool dripping from their wet tongues. They run around and bark before both coming to a screeching halt and pushing out the largest, most disgusting piles of shit I've ever seen. They look like dinosaur dumps and the thought of me picking these piles of shit up every day in our backyard fills me with dread.

'Oh, these must be the puppies' parents, look how cute they are,' says Rod as he opens the gate and makes his way over to the litter of puppies in a separate enclosure.

These beasts are not cute! They look like my sleep-paralysis demons charging towards me, desperate for human flesh and blood. We make our way over to the litter of puppies and I look up at Rod's face and my heart sinks. He's so happy and excited as he gazes down at the yelping pile of dirty little puppies rolling around in the enclosure. I must look like Cruella De Vil in this moment, glaring at the puppies with pure hatred. I just can't wait to get out of there.

'The puppies won't be ready for a new home for a couple more weeks,' the breeder says. Rod plays with the litter for another few minutes and then we jump in the car and head back to Newcastle.

On the drive to Rod's I'm incredibly torn. I feel like a total hypocrite because I'm the biggest preacher of following your dreams and here I was about to tell Rod I didn't want him to fulfil his. What's more, my big dream was still stirring me. I realise once we reach Newcastle, I need to be honest with him about my plans to live and work in America. Rod has known this was my dream but I think he's assumed now we're in love that I've had given up on it. This is not the case at all.

Rod has his mortgage broking business that he's built from scratch and it's going great. He's making more money than he's ever made before, has a brand-new car and no debt, and is much more successful than most people his age. Just before we met, Rod had started building his own home and the plan is to get his dream dog when the house is finished. Rod's whole life is here. Friends, family, home, career – it's not even feasible that he'd give all that up and follow me to America.

I'm so confused and don't want either of us to get hurt. We've been planning on moving into Rod's new place together, which Rod keeps calling 'ours'. It's definitely time to be honest with him about my true intentions.

As we reach his place, start putting together a lazy Sunday lunch while chatting, and then the conversation trails off. I'm shitting myself and so scared of the repercussions of what I will say next. I don't even know what I am going to say – but I think back to that moment on the plane, gazing at the Hollywood sign and swearing to return, and remember how determined I felt.

'I need to tell you something,' I say. Rod looks back at me with concern.

'You can tell me anything. What's the matter?'

This is the moment I've been dreading for the six months we've been together. I need to find the courage for this. I'm so deeply in love with him, and we're in the process of building our future together here in Newcastle, but I have this intense inner drive for something greater for us both.

Tears start to fall, and as I'm wiping them away I say, 'My dream is to still move to America.'

Rod's jaw hits the floor, and he just looks at me for what feels like an eternity. He then begins to tear up. *OMG what have I done.* I feel sick to my core. *Is he going to be furious and break my heart? Are we going to break up and he'll never speak to me again?*

I quickly jump back in and say, 'Mate, you know I've always dreamed of living in LA. I really don't want to let that dream go.'

I have a sudden epiphany, what Oprah calls an 'Aha! moment'.

'But that dream has changed,' I continue. 'You're my dream too now and I want you to come to America with me.'

Rod stands there looking back at me, completely stunned.

I'm sure he has a million different scenarios running through his head. After only a few months of dating I can tell Rod is a perfectionist. He always needs to be in control and have a solid, thought-out plan. My outrageous idea has thrown him.

He takes a deep breath and a smile appears on his face. 'Okay,' he says. 'Let's make it happen, together.'

I can't believe what I'm hearing. I am Hannah Montana in this moment, getting the best of both worlds. I can pursue my ultimate dream and do it with my Prince Charming by my side!

I'm so grateful Rod would do this for me. I know how much the life he has built for himself here in Newcastle means to him. I can't believe how lucky I am to have the love and support of this man.

'Are you sure?' I ask, worrying he might regret it.

'If someone had asked me this morning, I would have said there was no way I could just leave everything here, but as soon as you asked me, I just knew. You're the most important thing to me and I want to be with you, whether that's here or in LA.'

Tears of happiness and sheer love spring into my eyes. Turns out my perfectionist Prince Charming has had an epiphany of his own!

The next few weeks are filled with excitement and dreaming together about our hopeful future. Rod's new house is complete and we need to live in it for six months before we can rent it out and move to America. It's officially move-in day. The house is, of course, perfect. We have our own walk-in wardrobe, a cute bathtub for our date-night bubble baths and also a backyard to lay around in the sun together on those hot summer afternoons.

This is the first time I've lived with a boyfriend, and it feels amazing and liberating. Rod and I are so similar (apart from choice of dogs), and it feels like I've just moved into heaven with my soulmate. This is the first time in my life I've ever had the privacy to do whatever I want with the man of my dreams. We don't waste a second and the next few months are filled with us walking around the house naked 24/7, having sex in every room and cooking dinner in the nude. We're always sunbaking naked on the grass in our backyard, making love on the living-room sofa, and even dancing naked up and down the hallway after a few drinks on the weekends. It feels like we've embarked on our own sexual revolution. We're so comfortable with each other and having the ability to live out all our sexual fantasies without any worries or interruptions is so freeing. Our sex life is monumental. Our days consist of making love, working out and daydreaming about when we move to America in a few months.

Mum has always been our biggest champion. She came over to the house on our move-in day and gave us a housewarming present of matching rainbow tea towels. And then the following week, matching rainbow beach towels. To be honest it seems like every time we catch up with Mum or she drops by she comes bearing gifts, always in the rainbow theme. Rainbow coffee mugs, rainbow doormat and a rainbow notebook. The list goes on and on. She is so proud of me and happy I have found someone who makes me happy.

Life is perfect.

Well, almost. I just wish Rod's family were around to help celebrate our new life together. All Rod has ever wanted is to be loved and supported by his family for who he truly is. I can shower him in as much love as humanly possible, but I feel like my love for him contributes to his family's distaste for us both. I find we regularly catch ourselves riding this incredible high and then when we realise the huge chunk of Rod's life that is missing, we come crashing down again.

His family's lack of support confuses me. I know in my heart we're both good people and that we can both go to bed of a night being proud of who we are. We treat others with respect and wholeheartedly support everyone in their right to live life in whatever way makes them happy. Our love for each other is making us both incredibly happy and it infuriates me that his family is oblivious to it. We decide to fill the next few months with nothing but positivity and love, and no one on planet Earth is going to destroy our bond.

15

ROD: YES!

Imagine an entire country, your home country, being asked to vote for or against you. An entire population of your peers urged to judge you and decide whether you should have the same rights as someone else. This is the shitshow we call the 2017 Australian marriage equality plebiscite.

This is the same year Tim and I fall in love. I know he's the one I want to spend the rest of my life with. He is to be my de facto, life partner or boyfriend for life, but it's not possible for me to call him my husband in our own country. The plebiscite is a joke. Our government thinks it's a good idea to spend millions of dollars on a NON-COMPULSORY vote to help them decide if they should legalise two people getting married. All it does is bring all the hateful homophobes to the surface to give their unwanted religious belief that anyone different to them will go to hell. It is dividing the nation, and causing conflict, hurt and anger from one side of our country to the other, and for some of us, it's personal.

My relationship with my family is as difficult as ever. I haven't spoken to any of my family since my epic blow-up with Dad. My family all know that I'm gay, but none of them accepts it, and none has bothered to come and meet the love of my life.

Social media right now makes me sick. There's so much hate and animosity around this stupid vote. Religious people are telling LGBTQIA+ people they're going to hell and LGBTQIA+ people are telling 'No' voters to fuck off and stop being so closed-minded. I don't need to wonder how my family will vote and I don't want to know. But I know I can rely on my best friend, Mitch. Can't I?

Mitch and I have been friends since school. Back then we hung out all the time and had each other's back in everything. We still have no secrets from each other. This is more than a friendship: he's my brother. He's my family when I feel I don't have a family anymore.

Mitch met a beautiful girl, Claire, and they've been living and working in Canada for the past two years. Even on opposite sides of the globe, my relationship with Mitch has remained as strong as ever. He's always looked out for me, even calling me in the middle of the night once when I drunkenly texted him that I was in a bad way.

Mitch and Claire have just come back from their adventure, and are staying at Claire's grandparents' house until they find a place of their own. I can't wait to get my best friend and brother back. I'm so excited to introduce him to my new man, Tim, because I know they will get along like a house on fire.

The day after they fly in, I'm so excited to go see them. Even though Mitch and I have been messaging a lot, I want to know everything about his time away and there's so much I need to catch him up on.

'Rodney!' he says when they come to the door.

I give him the biggest hug and say, 'You aren't allowed to leave for that long ever again.'

'I promise I won't,' he laughs. I give Claire a big hug too and we go inside. Sitting down in the lounge room, I ask them to tell me everything. Most of the things he told me about Canada while he was away were about how cheap the cocaine was and how hard they partied, and I want to know it all.

He looks over at me and says, 'Claire and I are gonna get back into church, hey.'

I'm a bit stumped. I wasn't even aware that Claire had been religious, but whatever.

'Oh, really? That's good, what makes you want to do that?' I ask them.

'The last few months in Canada we just got really over the partying and want to get grounded again, and we feel like church will be good for us,' he says.

'I'm happy for you guys,' I tell them. 'As long as you're happy.'

Mitch asks me what's been happening with me and I go on for the next half an hour about Tim and how much I love him. Mitch doesn't seem as excited for me as I would expect. *He's probably still jetlagged.* As I'm leaving, we tee up plans so they can meet Tim.

A few days later, Tim and I head off to meet Mitch and Claire for lunch. 'You're going to love Mitch,' I say, 'I think you two will get along so well.'

'I hope he likes me,' says Tim, 'it's a bit nerve-racking meeting someone who means so much to you.'

We arrive down at the café where we'd arranged to meet, overlooking the lake. Mitch and Claire are already seated at a table at the back. I wave. As we make our way over to them I notice Claire's staring down at the table and Mitch is struggling to look our way. *Something's up.*

They stand and give me a hug.

'Mitch, Claire, this is Tim,' I say proudly.

They say hi but the response is lukewarm, to say the least, as if they already don't like Tim.

'Are you still jet-lagged?' I ask by way of small talk and trying to get a read of the room. Conversation just isn't flowing. In fact it's awkward. Tim offers to go up to the counter to order. I don't blame him, I don't want to be sitting here either.

Mitch starts telling me about the church he and Claire are going to.

'You should come check it out too,' he says to me.

I laugh and joke, 'I think I'll pass. I don't think they'll approve if I bring my boyfriend along.'

Mitch doesn't smile. *WTF is going on?*

Tim comes back and tries his best to keep the conversation going. 'How long have you guys been together?' he asks.

'We only just started dating before we went to Canada,' Claire says, and doesn't expand.

Poor Tim has nowhere to go with this conversation.

Mitch creates more small talk. 'How's work? Do you still hang out with Jez? What gym are you going to?'

Really. We haven't seen each other in two years and this is what you want to know?

After lunch, we get up to leave and say our goodbyes, and there's a weird tension in the air. As Tim and I walk out to the car, my mind is blown by how uncomfortable and awkward everything was. I start to worry if it has something to do with their decision to go back to church.

Come September and the country is asked to vote Yes or No for marriage equality. Tim and I proudly promote our love and push the Yes vote across our social media and in our social circles.

In mid-October, the deadline to cast a vote, Mitch calls to ask me to go out for a beer with him. I've been pretty caught up with work and the Yes vote, and it's been a few weeks since we last hung out so I'm keen.

We meet at a local pub. From the second I see him, I know something's wrong. *Who's sick? Has he broken up with Claire? Who died?*

We grab a beer and sit down. Mitch has tears in his eyes, and I'm concerned for him. He looks at me and, stumbling over his words, says, 'You know I love you and I think Tim is great, right?'

Oh no.

'You know how I've been going back to church?' Mitch says nervously.

I don't respond but I'm sure my feelings are written on my face.

'I just want to let you know in person that I've voted no,' he says.

The noisy pub recedes and I try to comprehend what Mitch just said. He keeps talking, tripping over his words.

'I don't mind you and Tim being together, I just don't believe in same-sex marriage,' he tries. 'I'm okay with gay people, I just don't think it should be called "marriage".' I can hear the panic in his voice. 'Marriage is between a man and a woman and it's special.'

Still I say nothing. What did he expect? *Did he honestly think I wouldn't be offended by this?*

Mitch has been my biggest supporter. All I can think about are the things he's said to me since the day I came out. He'd proclaimed that nothing would make him prouder than to stand up next to me on my wedding day as my best man and watch me marry the man of my dreams. Then he attends church for a few weeks, and he puts himself on some kind of a pedestal over me. This is just not okay!

'Why didn't you come and talk to me about it first when you know how much this means to me?' I ask.

'I'm talking to you now. I knew that talking to you wouldn't change my decision.'

'The vote isn't even compulsory!' I say. 'So why did you feel the need to vote, knowing I feel this way about it? I still wouldn't understand why you don't support me but wouldn't be so mad if you just didn't vote. You know you can change your vote, Mitch. Are you going to change it?'

'No,' he answers.

'You're meant to be my best mate, Mitch,' I tell him.

I stand up from the table and he grabs my arm. 'I'm so sorry Rod, I didn't want to hurt you.'

'If you were really sorry, you would never have voted no in the first place.'

I walk out and leave him sitting in the pub by himself.

I honestly expect some form of apology or a message telling me he's made a mistake but I don't hear from him. A few weeks later, as if to rub salt on my wounds, I see on Facebook that he proposes to Claire. To make things worse, they have the audacity to invite me to their wedding.

They expect me to go and watch them utilise their right to marry as a straight couple after voting against my right to do the same!

Mitch reaches out to me a couple of times to see if there's a way to salvage our friendship. But with his views remaining as they are, I can't get past what he's done. He has hurt me more than my family ever did. They were at least up front with me from the get-go and stuck to their guns which, in a twisted way, I can respect. But Mitch has done a 180 and torn my heart out, all in the name of Christianity.

The day arrives for the result of the same-sex marriage plebiscite. Tim and I are both really nervous. This is such a huge deal for me; this vote has caused a lot of pain and I am so worried that our country may just be like Mitch and vote No. We're following live updates on Instagram in the afternoon, and hear that the result will be announced shortly. There's so much nervous energy in our house that I suggest we go for a drive.

'We need drinks,' I say. 'We're either celebrating today or drowning our sorrows.'

Tim agrees and we jump in the car to head to the shops. We're both a little off and just quiet.

'Are you okay?' I ask Tim.

'Yeah all good,' he replies, then asks, 'you don't actually think it will be a No, do you?'

'We just need to be positive, Tim.' I try to be reassuring even though all I can think about is Mitch and my family.

We arrive at the shops and it's minutes before the announcement. Our eyes are glued to our phone screens, watching this rally on Instagram Live and waiting for the announcement. It's heart-warming to see so many people at the rally, with rainbow flags and signs in support of the Yes vote.

I look over at Tim and reassure him one last time before the announcement. 'Whatever the result, I love you and no one can stop us from being together.'

'Fuck yeah,' Tim replies and gives me a little kiss. 'If our country won't recognise our marriage then fuck 'em, we'll get married somewhere where they do.'

To our utter joy, the Yes vote is passed; Australia has legalised same-sex marriage! It is an amazing day. Over 61 per cent of Australians voted Yes, a majority vote. While it's sad that over 38 per cent of the population voted No, likely including my family and best friend, this is a huge win for us and our community, and we need to celebrate the wins.

We practically skip into the shops to get our drinks. Nothing can dull our sparkle in this moment but looking around, we wonder if we're alone. An iconic moment in Australian history has just gone down ... and inside the shopping centre everything looks exactly the same, business as usual. I didn't expect a mardi gras parade, but everyone's acting like nothing's happened.

On the drive home, our town seems just the same, no one out on the street celebrating the result. Nothing has really changed for most of Newcastle, but for us everything has changed.

We excitedly talk over the top of each other: 'This is so incredible!' 'What an amazing day!' 'We're finally being recognised as equals!!'

We get home and waste no time cracking open our first drink to celebrate. We toast each other and the result, and Tim says, half-joking, 'I can't wait to marry you now.'

I say, 'I wonder which one of us will propose first?'

Tim goes, 'Ooohhh imagine how strange it will feel calling each other husband!'

My phone rings, and it's my friend Jez in Sydney. I put him

on speaker and we're welcomed by an already intoxicated voice screaming, 'It's a Yes, it's a YES!!'

'I know. How amazing is it!' I say.

Jez jumps in with 'Just sayin, I better be best man at yours and Tim's wedding!' and we all crack up laughing.

'Anyways gotta go party but love you both byeeeee!' Jez says, and we hang up so he can continue his celebrations.

I can't help but think in this moment how Sydney's celebrating in the streets and Newcastle, only two hours away, is a completely different world.

We decide to put a post on Instagram, telling the world about the Yes vote. It gets mostly positive comments which is a relief considering the nation had been at war over this vote. We received an overwhelming amount of messages of love and support from people all over the world.

Many people are also confused and ask things like: 'What's the postal vote?' 'Why didn't the government just legalise it?' 'I thought it was already legal in Australia, you guys are so far behind!' These questions are so valid, and we can't give them an answer. All this vote did was make LGBTQIA+ people feel 'less than' and put them up in front of the nation to be judged all over again. It simply shouldn't have ever been put to a vote. Love is Love and there should be equality for all.

But the important thing is that we won, we've got a lot to celebrate – and the consequences are starting to fully dawn on me.

My fairytale could actually come true.

We've been together only a short time but I've never been more certain of anything. I want to marry Tim.

How soon is too soon to ask him?

I am so in love with Tim. Whenever he's not around I miss him like crazy and when we're together, I feel a joy like no other.

It's a Thursday night in April 2018, and Tim's at work. A little while ago he quit the corporate job he hated to pursue a career in personal training, and he's working as a checkout chick at Woolies while he studies.

I decide it's time. I pick up the phone and call Jez.

'Can you come up to Newcastle this weekend?!' I can't contain my excitement.

'OMG WHY?'

'I'm going to ask Tim to marry me!'

I have to hold the phone away from my ear, Jez squeals so loudly. 'Great, so I'll call in sick on Friday and drive up from Sydney first thing. We need to go ring shopping!' We hang up but we send each other photos of rings we like and plan where we'll go to look for the right one.

As I screenshot rings and send them to Jez, I'm also texting Tim, asking him how his shift is going.

SHIT! I accidentally send a picture of the ring I love to Tim instead of Jez. In a state of panic, I message Tim straightaway and tell him that Jez is planning to propose to his boyfriend.

Tim trusts me and happily believes my lie. Why would he think otherwise?

When Jez gets to Newcastle we go ring shopping. At the first jeweller on our list, he struts in and declares, 'This is my best friend, he is proposing to a man and we need a ring that screams masculine with a little bit of gay.' The jeweller directs us to the male wedding bands and one catches my eye immediately – white gold with a line of subtle diamonds. I can't stop looking at it. It fits Jez's description to a tee, but this is the first jeweller we've been to so we keep looking.

Seven jewellers later, I still can't get past that first ring: it is the one.

I have the ring – now for the proposal. The most difficult part about this entire situation is that I don't know the rules. If I propose with a ring, does Tim get me one? Do we need to then get wedding bands and wear two rings? I decide to simply do what feels right.

That weekend I arrange for Jez and another friend, Dan, who happens to be an interior designer, to set up the backyard. We decide on a huge flower arch and fairy lights zigzagging all the way from the house to the back fence. They make a path of candles leading up to the archway and place a huge bucket of ice with champagne and glasses at the end.

Everything will be perfect. My challenge is going to be keeping Tim out of the house long enough for them to come around and set up.

How Tim doesn't know I'm up to something is beyond me. I lie through my teeth all day. I try so hard to keep him busy – we go for a walk, then a drink at a bar, then another walk, then a coffee. Tim keeps telling me he just wants to go home, snuggle and watch a movie. Meanwhile I'm texting the boys for updates. Finally, they advise me they're done.

Now for the hardest part: I need to get home, change and be ready with the ring in hand under the flower arch. On the drive home, Dan calls as we'd planned, asking us over for a drink. I know Tim doesn't want to, but I immediately say yes and end the call. I explain to Tim that we'll just go for one drink and then go home. Being a liar is hard work.

We go to Dan's and after one drink I fake a phone call and go into another room; when I come back out I tell Tim I need to go to a client's house to get some documents signed. I ask Jez if he can bring Tim home soon. Tim doesn't protest.

I rush home, get all suited up, spray myself with cologne and head out the back. I grab my bluetooth speaker and cue up the song we fell in love to, 'Beauty and the Beast' by Ariana Grande.

My phone dings; it's Jez telling me they're around the corner. I make sure all the candles are lit and the fairy lights are on, put the ring in my pocket and take my place under the flower arch. I'm a ball of nervousness and excitement. This feeling reminds me of the first day I met Tim and I just can't wait to ask him to be my husband.

I hear Tim come home. 'Hello, hello!' he yells as he makes his way through the house. 'Please don't scare me,' he begs. (Scaring Tim is something I do often.) Meanwhile Jez sneaks into the backyard, ready to capture this special moment on his phone.

As Tim approaches the back door, I push play so he'll hear our song when he steps out into the perfect romantic setting.

He takes one step out the back, looks at me in my suit and yells, 'WHAT THE FUCK!' Jez has begun to film – yes, our romantic engagement video starts with this. With his hand over his mouth, Tim walks over to me with tears in his eyes. I get down on one knee and begin.

'Tim, I love you with all of my heart; you fill that part of me that has been missing my entire life. When I met you, my life became whole. You're my best mate and soulmate, and I cannot imagine doing life without you. Will you marry me?'

Without hesitation he screams, 'Yes, of course yes, OMG!'

With news of our engagement circling all over social media and now rumours of Tim and I moving to the other side of the world going around, I receive a message from my sister Emma inviting me over for dinner with her and her husband, Ben. She adds, 'We'd like to talk to you.'

About what, I think to myself and then write back, 'Hey Em, can I ask where you stand? Are you able to love and support me and my relationship or do you have the same stance as the rest of the family? If I can be brutally honest, I can't handle any more hurt and disappointment from my family so if you can't support me for me, then I'm not coming for dinner. I miss ya Em, and I want nothing more than for you to meet Tim.'

My phone rings immediately. 'I hate texting,' says Emma. 'Ben and I have been talking and we've decided that we'd like to meet Tim, but we want you to come for dinner yourself on Thursday so that we can talk to you alone first. Then we can have you both around next week so we can meet Tim.' This is the closest thing I've had in a long time to even a hint of family relationship so I agree.

Thursday rolls around; their house is a forty-minute drive away and I talk to Tim on speaker phone the entire way there. I'm trying to remain positive but have no idea how this dinner is going to go. Tim reassures me as I'm pulling up, 'Mate, I love you, and you'll be fine. And if they give you any shit, just get up and leave.' We hang up, I get out and head up to the house.

Okay, here we go. I take a deep breath and knock. Emma opens the door and I'm greeted by their dog Molly jumping all over me. We walk into the lounge room and take a seat on the lounge next to the fireplace. Ben offers me a beer and I say yes. *I'm definitely going to need this.*

We're all quiet for a moment and then Emma looks over at me and begins to cry. 'Rod, we want you here tonight because we love you and miss you so much.' She takes a breath and tries to compose herself. 'Ben and I are so sorry, Rod. We should've been there for you when you needed us and we want you back in our lives, and that includes Tim.'

I'm trying to hold it together; it's so hard to see Emma break down like this.

'Do Mum and Dad know you're talking to me?' I ask, trying not to get caught up in the emotion of it all.

'Yes, we actually told them last night that we were going to reach out to you to make peace.'

Tears roll down my face at this and my feelings all bubble to the surface.

Ben also begins to cry. 'Mate, you know I had a rough upbringing, being brought up in foster homes, so I know what it feels like to not have a family.' The tears stream. 'I know what you must have been going through and we're so sorry we haven't reached out sooner … we are so sorry.'

'I am so tired of crying, I am so tired of fighting,' I say, and we are a collective blubbering mess. Both Emma and Ben get up and wrap their arms around me and tell me again how much they love me. This is all I have been craving from my family.

We have a great dinner together after that and for the first time I feel like I've made a step towards mending things with my family.

The following week Tim comes up for dinner and we all get on fabulously. Ben and Tim hit it off and seem like they've been best mates for years.

A few days pass and Emma calls to tell me that she's spoken to Mum and Dad and told them that we've made up and that Tim's amazing, but it still isn't enough to convince my parents.

Or is it?

My phone dings not long after with a text from my dad. My guts start churning. 'Rod, can you meet me at the car park near our house this afternoon around 4? I need to talk to you.' We haven't spoken in months and I know Emma and Ben have been talking to Mum and Dad, so I hope it's positive. *The car park is literally thirty seconds from their house and it doesn't seem odd to meet there because it's neutral territory and every conversation in their home lately has turned into a fight.*

I reply, 'I don't mind meeting you Dad, as long as the conversation is positive because I don't have it in me for another argument or negative conversation.' Just like Emma, he calls.

I pick up and he says, 'This shit has gone on for too long and we need to sort it out, mate. It's tearing me apart.'

'It's tearing me apart too, Dad. I never wanted this.'

When I get there, Dad's already parked and waiting. I park next to him and he winds down his window and asks me to hop in his car.

I get in and he turns to me. 'I don't want to fight with you anymore mate, it's killing me and I just want my son back,' Dad says and he begins to cry. He honestly looks defeated.

'I want that more than anything Dad, but I'm not going to change who I am to make this happen. You've probably heard Dad, I'm engaged, I'm happy, I am so in love with Tim and we're moving to America. If you want to fix things, that means welcoming Tim into our family as well.'

Dad is surprisingly handling things pretty well. 'Mate, for me it's not even the gay thing anymore. Look, it's not the life I wanted for you as your dad, but it was your lack of respect towards us and the way you spoke to us; you told us that we were dead to you, mate. You had girlfriends in school and out of school, you wanted to go live in Africa at a Christian orphanage. It was so up and down, we didn't know what to think,' he says.

'Dad, I've known something was different about me since I was a kid. Growing up it was torture but you and Mum just didn't listen to me.'

'Mate, I want to put it all behind us and move on, can we do that?' he asks.

'Where is Mum, shouldn't she be here?' I say. He tells me he wanted to talk to me first.

'Does she even know you're here, Dad?'

He assures me she does. He calls her and asks her to meet us. When she arrives shortly after, Dad and I get out of the car and greet her. I give her a kiss on the cheek and can tell she's nervous.

'I've told Rodney we want to make things right,' Dad tells Mum. I jump in and tell Mum exactly what I told Dad – that Tim and I are a package deal.

Mum and Dad look at each other and Mum blurts out, 'No, you can't call me and expect me to just come here and all of a sudden be okay with this!'

'Why did you guys want to meet me then?' I ask, totally confused. 'There's no other way that this relationship is going to be mended. I'm happy and I'm marrying Tim whether you like it or not.'

'I just can't, I'm sorry, I'm a Christian and you know that, Rod,' Mum declares. 'You know what the Bible says about homosexuality. I just can't.'

I go to walk off to my car and Dad stops me, teary-eyed. He turns to Mum and says as tears roll down his face, 'He is our son.'

Mum just says, 'I need time to think and pray about this.'

So that's it. We all get back in our cars and drive off.

On my way home, I try to justify their reaction by telling myself they were raised in a different time or that they've been blinded by their Christian faith, but it's no excuse. All I'd been craving for the longest time was to hear my parents say, 'I am so proud of you.' Sure, they tell me they love me, but I don't feel it; at what point is that love enough to outweigh their beliefs and opinions?

Would they prefer I grow old alone and miserable or marry a woman, only to hurt her in the future?

16

TIM: Meeting the parents

Rod gets a message from his parents, Gary and Lee. 'We're on our way. We will be at your house in ten minutes.' *OMG.* is this really happening? Or is this a crazy dream and any second I'll wake up screaming in a pool of sweat?

When they told Rod they would come and visit, I hadn't quite believed it would happen, but now Gary and Lee are on their way to our house to meet me for the first time. I'm incredibly uncomfortable and frustrated about it, as I have a lot of built-up anger towards them. Rod texts back 'Ok see you soon' and I begin pacing up and down the hallway, trying to calm myself. I'm freaking out because I'm so nervous but I'm also angry because I've had to witness their lack of acceptance for their son's true self. My family has been amazing and enveloped me with love and acceptance, while Rod's has been the complete opposite. I've been a shoulder for Rod to cry on so many times, so naturally I'm defensive. But I'm also hopeful that tonight might be the very first step in rebuilding that shattered past.

'Do you want a vodka?' Rod yells out from the kitchen.

I Usain Bolt into the kitchen. 'Make it a double.'

We cheers each other and down our drinks. We want his parents' love and acceptance so bad it physically hurts.

The car pulls into the driveway and we hear footsteps towards the door.

'THEY'RE HERE!' Rod yells as he frantically tidies up the kitchen and makes his way to the front door. I take a deep breath and picture the ways this can play out, from happy hugs to a full-blown *Real Housewives* argument, with tables flipped and glasses of wine thrown.

Rod opens the door and greets his mum and dad with a hug, then welcomes them into our home. I need to calm down as I don't want to stuff this up by stumbling over my words and making a fool of myself right off the bat. Neither do I want to seem too casual or upbeat. Gah! I reach out and shake Gary's hand with a nice strong grip like my dad always taught me. I want to show him that I'm just a normal bloke who happens to be in love with his son.

'Hi Gary, I'm Tim,' I say, maintaining eye contact and a firm grip.

'Nice to meet you, mate,' he says, in a friendly manner that has me pleasantly taken aback.

Rod's mum is next. 'It's so nice to meet you Lee, I'm Tim,' I say, as I give her a warm, welcoming hug. Mums always give the best hugs and Lee's feels just as comforting as a hug from my very own mum.

'It's nice to meet you, darlin',' she whispers in my ear. I am stumped! They seem lovely. *What is going on? Okay so this isn't so bad and at least the awkward hellos are out of the way, but oh no, now it's time to chat.*

Rod leads us to the living room, and we all sit down on the lounge together. I'm getting nervous again, trembling and sweating, although the vodka I smashed minutes ago is definitely taking the edge off. I hate confrontation at the best of times.

Small talk ensues. 'How was your day?' 'What are your plans for the weekend?' 'How nice has the weather been?!'

After the ice is broken Rod's mum and dad turn the conversation to serious matters.

'Tim, we want you to know this was never about you personally, but it's just not what we believe in. We feel two men shouldn't be together,' says Rod's mum. I picture a warm hug followed by a knife in my heart. She's basically saying they don't have an issue with me but are completely against everything I stand for and represent, even down to my DNA.

'We want to start rebuilding our relationship but we can't come to your engagement party,' Rod's dad says. 'This is very new to us and we don't want to be judged by people attending your party.'

Even though I would love for all of Rod's family to be at our upcoming engagement party (which will double as our 'Going to live in America' party), it didn't feel like that was really on the cards anyway. Baby steps. The night is a success overall. We clear the air and, for the first time, they listen to Rod talk about how he's felt all these years. Gary then wraps up the conversation with some optimistic final words. 'We miss you, Rod, and we really want to move forward and make things better between us all.'

They aren't what I expected at all. They aren't angry, mad or yelling, just really nice. Gary is so easy to talk to and it feels like I am almost talking to my own dad. He is incredibly genuine and super friendly. Lee is so likeable as well. Her laugh is contagious and, apart from the obvious religious stuff, it seems like we have truck loads in common. At one point I take off my engagement ring to show her and she grabs it out of my hands and tries it on.

'Oh it looks lovely, darlin',' she says.

We arrange to meet up for a coffee in a few days and I'm shocked to realise I'm actually looking forward to that. I enjoy their company and, aside from the clash of views in regard to our sexuality – a pretty fundamental point of course – I find them to be really amazing people.

This could finally be the breakthrough we've been waiting for. After they leave, Rod and I make the decision to focus on the positive. Okay, they're not totally over the moon for us, but they're wanting to take steps forward. This is fantastic.

Meanwhile, our move to the States is something to focus on. After a few weeks of legwork we're both able to secure jobs at an Australian-owned gym in West Hollywood. We're also able to pay bond and rent for a cute little apartment right in the heart of West Hollywood. We even go to the extent of planning our Las

Vegas wedding in the same chapel Britney Spears got married in. Our future is looking bright, and I can't wait to introduce Rod to my fantasy gay Wizard of Oz world. In my mind we'll be two Dorothies heading along the yellow-brick road on the greatest adventure of our entire lives.

Personally, I've never been in a better place than I am right now. I've ditched the soul-destroying job, and I'm on top of my alcohol problem and eating disorder. After I came out, I'd felt a huge weight lift off me, which I'm sure was the main contributor to my toxic drinking and dangerous food issues.

Meeting Rod had also helped silence my inner demons and negative impulses. Being able to confide in someone who I wholeheartedly trusted helped release a lot of the pent-up anger and resentment that had been festering over the years. They say 'A problem shared is a problem halved' and that's exactly how I felt with Rod. There are still days when the toxic patterns from my past resurface but now that I have a warrior in Rod who'll go into battle by my side, the war within myself is a lot easier to conquer.

Heading to the States feels like a fresh start for us both, a chance to shed the baggage of our pasts and leave behind all the negative childhood memories, all the family and friendship breakdowns, and all the judgement we still encounter from people who don't support our love. The fact that Rod has now jumped on the bandwagon with me just makes it so much sweeter.

We fully invest ourselves in planning our fantasy American life together. We sell pretty much everything we own, cars, appliances, furniture, and are left with basically just the clothes on our backs.

Our combined engagement–farewell party is a blast. The house is filled with balloons, support and affection. My entire extended family come, along with our closest friends. The most hopeful thing of the whole night is when Rod's sisters Emma and Kelly, along with their husbands Ben and Paul, come and celebrate. It warms my heart to see Rod's siblings slowly coming to terms with his sexuality, and softens the still considerable blow that his parents decided not to come.

After the celebration, the only thing left to do is head to the American Consulate in Sydney and collect our work visas. We arrive in Sydney on the day of the consulate meeting and practically burst through the doors to the consulate, we are so eager to secure our two visas.

A consular representative takes us through to an office and we sit down ready to take this giant leap. The room feels cold, and the large number of stern-looking security guards make it feel more like a high-security prison than an outpost of diplomacy. Huge American flags are draped in every corner, and a picture of Donald Trump stares down at us.

Eventually it's our turn.

'Next!' says the attendant impatiently, like we've been holding him up. We sheepishly approach the window and beam Disneyland smiles that we hope make us desirable candidates for a visa, while really I feel like vomiting, pissing and shitting myself all at the same time.

'Hi,' we both say breezily as we hand over our stack of documents.

'We're here to provide the documentation for our working visa,' I say, trying to sound efficient. I don't know why I'm so scared; we have everything in order and we've even already got jobs lined up. I guess it's because so much is riding on this and I don't want anything to fuck it up for us.

The guy takes our documentation and flicks through it, scanning his eyes over every page. As he finishes reading the last one he takes a deep breath, hands them back to us and declares, 'You don't qualify for the working visa.'

My head screams, *What the fuck are you fucking talking about for fuck's sake?!* But I say, 'Excuse me, sir? How is this possible?'

'You don't meet the requirements,' he says, looking over our shoulders for the next dream to crush. We can't believe what we're hearing. How can this be happening?

We jump back in the car, heartbroken and embarrassed, and start the journey home. How could we have been so naive? Our prospective American employer has misled us. On multiple occasions he told us how easy the visa process is and how they've dealt with so many Australians before us.

We're furious about this, but hopeful the employer can sort it out. We try calling him from the car multiple times but keep getting voicemail. He finally picks up, we relay our story and he just says, 'It's not my problem. If you can get a visa, you have the job, if you can't, then too bad.' He's certainly changed his tune. He'd assured us that our qualifications would transfer to the United States. We even have paperwork from the American side saying we're eligible and our jobs are accepted.

We have been completely fucked over. On the drive home we call an immigration lawyer to get some advice and guidance. This only makes us feel worse as they confirm that without us both completing a full university degree in exercise physiology, we'll be unable to secure the visa. We have sold all our belongings and invested most of our money in securing an apartment in West Hollywood, but it's impossible for us to get there.

The dream is over.

Returning to Newcastle, we feel so devastated and embarrassed. We're now unemployed – I'd chucked my job in and Rod had wound down his mortgage broking business so we could go to the States – and everyone knows that our big plans have been derailed.

But we're not quitters, nor the type of people to wallow. We've been through worse and know that together we can overcome anything. We're still passionate about health and fitness, for ourselves as well as work, so we brush ourselves off and secure jobs at a local group fitness studio. We're at least doing something we love but the money is atrocious, and we feel as though we're getting taken advantage of by the owner. We both work ridiculous hours and put in an enormous amount of time and energy. The whole environment is toxic, and we're under immense financial pressure. We can't keep living like this.

One drunken night, we have another Oprah 'Aha! moment' while scrolling through our joint Instagram account. After Rod and I got together, I'd posted a few sexy pictures of us and we noticed that the photos with both of us in them did much better than the solo ones.

We're having a few drinks, checking out other profiles, when we stumble across OnlyFans, a platform where people charge a monthly subscription fee for exclusive pictures and videos. We quickly realise we can post pretty much exactly what we're currently posting on Instagram on OnlyFans and get paid for it. It seems way too good to be true, but we're desperate. After a few more shots of vodka, we take the plunge and create an OnlyFans account.

We decide on a monthly fee of $10 and set the app to send us a notification email every time a new subscriber signs up. Next we upload some raunchy content we have already saved on our phones. Moments later, my phone dings. We have a subscriber already! Then there's another ding, and another, and another, every few seconds. For the rest of the night and into the early hours of the morning my phone keeps dinging. We can't believe what's happening. Every alert is another $10 a month for us, and over the course of the next few days our monthly subscriptions grow to a point where we're making thousands of dollars for something we were already giving away for free.

We quickly come to a crossroads: we can either keep working like slaves at our personal training jobs or post a few photos a week on OnlyFans and quadruple our weekly income. It's not rocket science; we need money to survive, and OnlyFans is providing it a lot easier and quicker than we could have ever imagined. We feel like we've won the sexy lottery and we quit the fitness studio. Oh how good that feels, having our financial independence and not being slaves to our boss.

The more X-rated our content is, the more the subscribers flow in and the more lucrative this business venture becomes. The fans can't get enough, and neither can we. We step the content up a notch and become as raunchy as humanly possible. The only rule we have set in place is 'fake it till we make it', which means we stage photos and videos to simulate sex, but we don't actually do it. We also promise each other we'll never show our penises, balls or actual assholes. Apart from that, we can be as sexually explicit as our hearts desire.

In the space of a couple of weeks, we become swept up in the want and need to shock our subscribers with new and exciting content. OnlyFans is perfect for us: not only does the platform give us validation like Instagram does, but it also puts ridiculous amounts of money in our pockets. Desperate people do desperate things, and at this low point in our lives we are willing to do whatever it takes to get us back on track. There's also the thrilling aspect of how liberating this is for us both after spending so much of our lives stuffed in the closet.

We're exposed to even more temptation when we discover the 'Tip' feature on our OnlyFans account. This allows our fans to message us directly and request random pictures and videos to satisfy their personal fetishes and kinks. We're bombarded with requests and become obsessed with fulfilling our fans' outrageous demands – but only for a significantly higher price. Messages like, 'Send me a photo of your feet', 'I want a video of you both in the shower together', 'Send me a video of you massaging each other naked' and 'I want a photo of your asses' are just the tip of the iceberg. We're aware that it might seem humiliating, gross and like we've lost all our morals, but these people are offering us hundreds of dollars; sometimes we make a thousand dollars in an hour. We're still so humiliated from the crash and burn of our West Hollywood dream and time at the fitness studio that we would probably sell our souls to the devil to get our lives back on track.

That is, until I receive a phone call from my mum.

'Are you doing porn now?' she asks, right off the bat.

'No, I promise we're not,' I reply, as my brain scrambles to catch up. Someone has obviously told Mum about our OnlyFans account.

Mum is very understanding, and she never gets angry or yells; however, she is clearly disappointed in me. 'I just don't want you to do something you'll look back on and regret one day,' she says.

After reassuring Mum it's not hardcore porn and talking our OnlyFans down as much as possible, I calm the situation.

However, I can tell she's still horrified by the idea. From her voice, I get the impression she's heard we've been doing full-blown pornographic pictures and anal penetration videos online.

Regardless of what it is or isn't, it doesn't feel good in my heart and soul. From the moment I get the panicked call from Mum, OnlyFans isn't sitting right with me anymore.

Also, seeing as Rod's family have begun to show signs of mending their broken relationship, doing something like this isn't likely to help that situation. Here we are slowly taking steps to reconcile with Rod's family while at the same time posting a suggestive photo of us soaping our asses up in the shower together on our OnlyFans account.

What the hell are we thinking?

We begin to see things more clearly. Sure, selling raunchy pictures and videos of ourselves online is lucrative, but we certainly don't want our families thinking we're porn stars now, and no amount of money is worth risking our own relationship. We've dedicated so much of our time to OnlyFans and making sexy content that ironically our sex life has become non-existent.

So after a month on OnlyFans we delete the page. We both have much bigger dreams and aspirations for what we want to achieve in life, and as hard as it is to walk away from the money, we do. Rod decides to relaunch his mortgage broking business and sets up an office from home so I can help with the admin side. Rod hates mortgage broking, and doing the paperwork is a mindless job, but it pays well and we need the money. We need a stabiliser.

From this point onwards, we promise each other we'll start pursuing all the goals we want to tackle in life together. If we have a positive, never-give-up attitude and a willingness to hustle, anything is possible. Amazing things are just around the corner for us, we just know it.

We're about to get married, after all!

I am over the moon in the weeks leading up to our wedding. The fairytale is finally, FINALLY about to come true.

I'm not sure if I was just born a daydreamer or if it's something I started doing to escape my reality, but it happens a lot (sorry, Rod). One of my biggest fantasies growing up was that I'd meet my Prince Charming and we'd live happily ever after in a land of unicorns and rainbows ... ooh there I go again! In my imagination, I took Cinderella's place and met the man of my dreams.

Let's face it, there aren't many Disney movies where Prince Charming gets back on his horse, heads to the next kingdom over and finds an equally eligible prince to marry. In fact ... there's none. So while in a way I was waiting for my *Brokeback Mountain* adventure or to be swept off my feet by Jack Dawson in *Titanic*, I had mostly come to terms with forgetting about that kind of future.

But Rod swept me off my feet. He was the knight in shining armour (well, footy shorts and a singlet) I had wanted. He gave me a renewed sense of hope that my glorious big gay future might materialise. It was as if the Gay Gods had answered my prayers.

From the second we met I felt liberated, able to fully be myself. His winning combination of genuine personality, sexy good looks and heart of gold makes him my perfect match. When I'm around him, I feel completely at peace with myself and with life. We're deeply connected, way beyond just physical attraction. How you make others feel about themselves says a lot about you, and Rod makes everyone feel like a somebody. This to me screams *husband material.*

I've been prepared to marry Rod since almost the second I met him (if that had been legal!). We've created ourselves a love bubble and tried not to let anything come between us – as hard as that seems at times. I know I love him, but I also know we can't be together completely while other important people in his life are holding back. What's the point of our union being recognised by law if my beloved's family want no involvement?

My family share some of the Christian values of Rod's but with opposite results. My Aunty Jenza, who will be marrying us, has been a devoted Christian her entire life. She's deeply religious and has even put her job as a Catholic school teacher on the line to be a part of the wedding. This is going to be her first time legally marrying a couple, so for her to choose her nephew's gay wedding is iconic ... snaps for Aunty Jenza.

Don't get me wrong, we're having truckloads of fun planning the wedding, but it's interspersed with the sadness of knowing not everyone will be part of it – not through distance or circumstances, but because they don't want to be.

There are times during the wedding preparation where it feels like an emotional tug of war. One second, I'm overwhelmed with happiness and the next devastated by words, judgements and homophobic hostility.

My emotions reach boiling point when Rod's other siblings inform us that his nieces and nephews won't be permitted to attend the wedding. His siblings view our wedding as improper and unsuitable for children. Exposing their children to a same-sex wedding could be so damaging that it would have a lasting negative influence on their young and impressionable minds! What the hell?

I have seen firsthand Rod's strong and beautiful relationship with his nieces and nephews. He is genuinely such an amazing uncle, so much so that I have glimpses of our future with our own kids. This news made me sick – how dare they! Not only are we judged for our choices, now we're labelled bad role models grouped with people not suitable to be around children, like paedophiles and sex offenders. How can same-sex marriage be legal and yet people still think this way?

I always try to be the most energetic, fun, positive and determined person in the room. As a gay kid you have to have so much spirit and positive energy just to get through tough situations and pick yourself up after being knocked down so many times. You spring into a situation and try to make other people comfortable and happy, overcompensating for *their* negativity. It's so draining and exhausting and sometimes you just have to take yourself away and recharge. And other times you're just crushed, especially when the person you hold dearest is hurting so much.

I just want to say to Rod's family, 'I will love your son and your brother more than anyone else could,' and surely that's all you need from your son's life partner. What do you think is wrong with me? What's wrong with us? Am I not good enough for your son? Their response to our wedding feels like a mirror reflecting and amplifying the anxieties and lack of self-worth I had battled for so many years. They gave validation to the demons that had always swirled around in my head.

As a gay man, the most hurtful thing in the world is when you're made to feel like there's something mentally wrong with you, that you are 'less than' because of some genetic code you had no part in designing. Again, the unworthy, outcast feelings returned, and I was back in the school yard, that weird kid that everyone made fun of.

A few weeks before the wedding, Rod and I are sitting in the loungeroom when he gets a call from the hire company – the white chairs we've selected for our beach ceremony are no longer available. He slams his phone down on the coffee table so hard that it bounces.

'I told you the cheaper chairs were a bad idea,' he snaps. 'Now we have to start from scratch and find a new hire company on short notice and we're totally screwed!'

His fuse is short at the moment, and I'm often on the receiving end but we both know it's nothing to do with the chairs or the colour of the flowers or where a certain guest is sitting.

'Mate, it's okay,' I say, leaning over and putting my hand on his knee. 'We have lots of options,' I tell him calmly. His surprisingly still functional phone lights up again. It's his dad, and he wants us to come over.

It's the latest round in a see-sawing of indecision from them – 'We're willing to consider'/ 'We will come but … / 'It's nothing personal but we just don't think it's right'/'We *should* be able to make it'. Poor Rod is living on his nerves, never knowing when the next call will come to dash his hopes. Their support is the one thing missing in our fairytale.

17

ROD: Our happily ever after

I walk towards the beach and from the peak of the dunes, I get my first glimpse of the setting for my day, our day. I can see everything, or at least I could see everything if my eyes weren't welling up.

'They're here,' Tim says, squeezing my hand. I'm so happy I could faint. The path to the beach is lined with trees, the surf club is on the left and the ceremony is set up in a secluded spot on the southernmost point of the beach near the rocks. Our whole wedding party walks behind us and everyone is beaming.

I go straight to Mum and Dad, who look even more nervous than me. I wrap my arms around them and give them both the longest hug and thank them for being here. This moment is something I have dreamed of my entire life. I never thought I would meet my Prince Charming, let alone have my parents there to walk me down the aisle and give me away to a man.

I walk Mum and Dad over to Tim's mum, Kathy, who has been our biggest supporter. She also believes in God but believes more powerfully in love. With a soothing voice she has always reassured me that my family would come around, and she always looked at my situation without judging me or my parents. They meet today for the first time and in true Kathy style she welcomes them like old friends.

We line up in the order that we are going to walk down the aisle, and Mum and Dad stand either side of me. The music starts, an acoustic version of 'Can You Feel the Love Tonight' from *The Lion King*, sung by Tim's cousin Amy. This song alone is enough to make anyone cry. Our party is led by Tim's gorgeous niece and nephews, Poppy, Winston and Eddie, followed by his brothers and a group of my closest friends. Tim goes before me holding his mum's hand, wearing the biggest smile I've ever seen. Then it's my turn, the moment I've been so nervous about, and Mum and Dad grip my hands. I know they're still not 100 per cent comfortable but, in this moment, I know they love me more than anything. I feel a sense of freedom like never before, an acceptance I've never felt. I can feel myself letting go of the hurt and pain I've endured over the years. Finally I feel right now that I'm able to forgive them and feel their forgiveness for the things I've said and done to hurt them also.

We've set up white chairs (yes, we managed to get another set) with a flower arrangement at the end of each row. We have a flower archway made from tree branches and white tulle. One hundred of our nearest and dearest are waving at us, blowing kisses, their faces full of joy. To the right is my family, who are all here, this is incredible. To the left is Tim's family, including his dad, Rocko, who looks so proud. Under the archway is Tim's Aunty Jenza, our celebrant.

It is time; we're about to get married. Tim and I kiss our parents and I make a point of telling Mum and Dad I love them. Simple words crossing a crater of differences and past conflict, words I have struggled with a lot over the past few years. They tell me they love me back and I believe them.

It is our wedding day and finally I feel like I belong again, I am part of my family again. What's even more spectacular is that my Tim is about to join our family too.

Our parents take their seats, and I grab Tim's hands and wait for Aunty Jenza to begin the ceremony. Holding Tim's hands, I look into his eyes. He doesn't need to speak; he just smiles and makes me feel safe and secure. He makes me feel like a king and I have never been surer of anything in my life. I love him and am about to become his husband.

Our vows are magical, and eerily similar, which cements how alike we are and how much we are meant to be together. Tim goes first. He doesn't need a microphone because he never has a problem being heard but Aunty Jenza gives him one anyway.

'Rod, the love I have for you in my heart is indescribable and I can't put into words how much you mean to me and how you have helped me become my true, authentic self. Growing up I was so scared of what my future looked like. I felt so different to everyone, alone and like I didn't fit in. I was never able to find someone who gave me reassurance that everything would be okay. I feel that with

you, and I know you are the one because now all that fear is gone.'

I am so glad my family is here to hear Tim's vows. I genuinely believe that will give them peace about the man he is and who I will be spending the rest of my life with.

When it comes time for my vows, I can hardly speak. 'I knew I should have gone first,' I say, choking back tears. Everyone laughs, which gives me a moment to compose myself.

'Tim, when you came into my world, I quickly realised you were the part of me that had been missing and for the first time in my life I felt pure happiness. You taught me what it was to love and be loved.

'I can't promise perfection or rainbows and fairies every single day, but what I can promise is that I will always be your best mate, I will always be by your side through thick and thin and I promise to keep dreaming big with you for the rest of our lives.

'I love you with all my heart and today I stand here the proudest man alive that I am so blessed to be the one to call you my husband and soulmate.'

Aunty Jenza pronounces us HUSBANDS and our guests erupt in celebration as we walk back down the aisle hand in hand. This is the proudest moment of my life. Tim runs over to his family and there are kisses and hugs all around. Tim then joins me with my family where Dad says to him, 'Welcome to the family, mate.' What makes this moment even more spectacular is that it's a Saturday afternoon on a public beach so there are heaps of bystanders watching two men get hitched and they're cheering and clapping along with our guests.

As we're getting our photos taken, I feel like I am floating. I'm so happy, without a negative feeling in sight. We are now husbands, a term that is going to take some getting used to. Strangers on the beach, even children, are coming up to congratulate us which is simply iconic.

We head back to the reception and are welcomed by the MC. One by one our wedding party is introduced, then finally it's our turn.

'Please welcome Tim and Rod Sattler-Jones!' Goosebumps!

'How good does that sound?' I say to Tim as we dance our way into the reception. To look around the room and see so many people, especially our families there supporting our wedding, is so incredible and liberating even if the guests have drunk most of our booze before we got there. Don't worry; we had Uncle Damo on standby for such an outcome and he races to the bottle shop to get more.

Tim's mum Kathy starts off the speeches. She loves to talk; if she got her way, she would have been the celebrant, and the MC, and would have given everyone's speech for them. She confidently walks up on stage with her pages ready. Tim's brothers are ready to cut her off is she goes too long. But everything she says is perfect and there is not a dry eye in the house. A few of Kathy's words seem to resonate with everyone in the building: 'Being able to celebrate together tonight, we are saying YES to LOVE. Today is a celebration of that love and commitment to each other. We are proud of both of you for being brave enough to be who you are.'

Then it's my parents' turn. I'm not sure where this will go. I've heard Dad's speeches at all my siblings' weddings and am curious to see what he will do. Mum stands up with him in support.

'Tim, in the short time we have known you, you have showed us love and friendship, and most of all respect, which Lee and I admire and love you for,' he says.

Did Dad just tell my new husband that he loves him? My heart is so full of joy I could burst.

'Rodney, we are incredibly proud of you, and want you to know that your mum and I love you deeply, always have and always will.' These are words I will take to my grave and that I have been longing to hear for years.

Our first dance, naturally, is to 'Beauty and the Beast' by Ariana Grande. It's the song that we slow danced to in the shower on one of our first dates and the song I had playing when I proposed to Tim. Then we have the honour of dancing with our mums, which is a special moment for us both. Mum and I just hold each other dancing, our eyes filling with tears. I tell Mum how much it means to me that she is here and tell her I love her again.

'I have always loved you, Rod,' Mum says, looking deep into my eyes. 'I am so proud of you and I promise nothing will ever get in the way of our relationship again. It has been a beautiful day.'

Our wedding day is simply perfect, and we then embark on the trip of a lifetime, flying out to the Maldives for our honeymoon the next morning. When we come back we'll bring our puppy, Diesel, into our family. As our Queen Miley Cyrus says, 'Life's a climb, but the view is great.' We know it's been worth the climb to find one another. We choose love over hate, and want to radiate positivity and kindness into the world and watch it manifest into something amazing. This Prince has found his Prince Charming and this is our Happily Ever After. It can't get any better than this, can it?

18

TIM: The Amazing Race Australia

It's a cold and wet Monday afternoon, and we're scrolling through Facebook when a random casting call catches our attention. The production company is looking for teams of two to take part in a 'travel adventure show'. We wonder, could this be *The Amazing Race*? *The Amazing Race* is one of our favourite TV shows; we both grew up watching it. Straightaway we agree that this opportunity has us written all over it. We thrive on spontaneous adventures, we're obsessed with travelling, we could do it together and the fact that there is a 'huge cash prize' for the winner is the cherry on top. We waste no time and quickly complete step one of the application process, which is a short question and answer document.

A week later we receive an email notifying us that we've been successful and can proceed to the next stage of casting. *OMG, how exciting is this?* Even at this initial stage we have high hopes and if nothing else, the process is an exciting.

The next stage requires us to provide a short video introducing ourselves, how we know each other and why we would be great contestants on this particular show. From the very beginning we promise each other that we'll be nothing but ourselves and if they like us, they like us and if they don't, it's their loss. With this in mind we get straight into making our video submission. We sit down on the couch, nervous and excited, and prop up our iPhone ready to film. Just before we hit record, we look at each other and realise 'Something is not right,' like Miss Clavel from the movie *Madeline*. Wardrobe! We're wearing boring black gym gear. This won't do it at all!

We want to catch the eye of the producers so we head to our wardrobe and start brainstorming. We usually wear matching outfits and decide to run with that for our audition video, picking out all the different options where we have an identical pair. Our matching faux-fur leopard-print jackets are iconic but don't seem like the most practical outfit for a 'Travel Adventure Show'. Our matching crop tops are eye-catching but have us showing a bit more skin than the producers may want. Delving deeper into the wardrobe, we strike gold. Like a beacon of Aussie bogan light shining through from the depths of the cupboard are two matching red and black flannelette shirts with the sleeves cut off. We immediately decide these are perfect and throw them on. Sitting back down on the couch, we hit record, complete our video and nervously send it off.

After another week passes and we receive a second email from the production company, notifying us that we have made it to the third and final round. The email tells us that this audition is split into two stages. Round one is a group challenge, after which only a select few will make it through to the panel interview with the show's executive producers. This seems very daunting, but we're so excited and proud to have made it to the final round and now even more determined to impress.

Arriving in Sydney on the day of our final audition, we are so motivated to make a positive impression on the producers. We want them to love us and are desperate to show our personalities and give them all an insight into who we are – without looking too nervous. We decide to wear our matching flannos once again to make sure we stand out, and to just have fun and not take it too seriously. Many other hopeful teams are also here at the final audition, all eager to secure a spot in this amazing travel adventure opportunity. As the teams wait nervously together in a holding room, the main casting producer enters and at the top of her lungs yells, 'Welcome, Racers!' Rod and I both freeze and look at each other. Racers? *We were right!*

'I want to congratulate you all for making it to the final round of auditions for *The Amazing Race Australia*,' says the producer. We are ecstatic, knowing that we're auditioning for our favourite show ever.

There are eleven other teams, all lined up waiting to be told what happens next. There are Beauty Queens, YouTubers, Father-and-Daughter teams, and Nurses, to name a few. And here we are looking like lumberjacks; surely nobody here thinks we're gay!

We're all given a team number – Rod and I are team number two – and the task is explained. It's a group challenge. The producers set us up at separate stations and we have to build a tower out of straws and playdough. We quickly realise that the challenge has nothing to do with the construction activity; it's more to see how we react with a camera floating around and coming up into our faces. We nail it. Our tower sucks and is practically falling over but we feel very natural in front of the camera.

Next, we are all lined up against the wall. One team at a time, we're asked to go out the front of all the other teams, facing a big light and camera, and explain to everyone why we should be picked and what we'll spend the prize money on. Some teams struggle and others absolutely nail it as if they've rehearsed hundreds of times. We haven't prepared anything, and it's our turn.

We bounce up and take our place. 'I am Tim, and I am Rod, and WE ARE THE NEWLYWEDS,' we say as we flash our matching wedding rings to the producers and the other teams. The room erupts in applause. I feel a huge transformation in this moment and can't help thinking back to the last time I spoke in front of a large group, at uni, when I was on the verge of a severe anxiety attack and had to get drunk in the car park just to get through it. I realise that through the combination of learning to love myself and coming out to the world, I've developed the self-worth and confidence I needed so desperately. In this moment I feel so powerful, as it's a complete 180-degree turn from the anxious, scared person I used to be.

'We think Australia and the world need more same-sex representation and not just the same old gay stereotype you normally see on TV shows,' Rod says to more applause.

'And we loved being able to get married so much that we'll spend the prize money on getting re-married in the White Chapel in Las Vegas where Britney Spears tied the knot,' I add. The room is in stitches laughing as the producer tells us to take our place back in the line. When all the teams are done, we're asked to go back to the waiting room while the producers decide who makes it to the panel interview. Fifteen minutes pass and then we're called back into the room. In my mind's eye, I am picturing American flags and a photograph of Donald Trump towering over us.

'We can do this,' I whisper in Rod's ear.

'We can do anything together,' he whispers back.

'If I call your team number,' says the producer, 'congratulations, you are progressing through today.' We grip each other tight. 'Team one, Team four.' *Oh no, she missed our number, we haven't made it.* 'Team seven, Team two.'

TEAM TWO! OMG YASSSS that's us, we've made it through! We're jumping up and down, one more hurdle left to go. The successful teams are told to go back to the waiting room to be called for the panel interviews.

After what feels like hours of waiting, it's finally our turn. We sit on stools in front of a panel of four intimidating producers. There are multiple cameras pointing at us, recording everything we say from the second we enter the room, along with huge bright lights beaming down on us. We sit there for the next thirty minutes answering every question under the sun. The producers want to know about everything. Our relationship, our families, what we fight about, pet peeves, what we're good at, what we're scared of. This is a full-blown interrogation. After the producers are satisfied, we leave and are told to return home; they will be in touch in the next few weeks to notify us if we're successful.

On the drive home we're optimistic but agree that we've given it our best shot and are proud and that we just had fun. In our minds, even if we don't make it, the fact that we stayed true to ourselves and did not put on a phony, false persona is all that matters.

Three weeks later we're sitting at home, funnily enough watching a previous season of *The Amazing Race*, when Rod's phone rings. 'Hi, this is Kim from *The Amazing Race Australia*, are you able to chat?'

He puts the phone on loudspeaker, and we try to act cool.

'Yes, of course,' we say.

'Are you sitting down?' she says.

This is it.

'I'm ringing to let you know that you have been selected as one of our lucky teams to take part in *The Amazing Race Australia*,' Kim says. We scream so loud Kim might have heard it even if she wasn't on the phone. We are going to race around the world in the hope of winning a huge $250,000 cash prize. After all the shit we've been through, this is just unbelievable. And I know in my heart that if we had let any of our previous problems break us or defeat us, there's no way we would have got this opportunity. If we hadn't stayed positive and enthusiastic, we would not have been picked.

In case you don't know it, *The Amazing Race* is an adventure reality game show in which teams of two people race around the world in competition with other teams. The race is split into different legs, with the teams required to conquer a range of varying challenges along the way in order to receive clues on their next destination of the race. The challenges are made up of Detours (a choice between two vastly different tasks each with their pros and cons) and Roadblocks (only one person from each team of two can participate). The challenges are based around the everyday cultural practices of the different countries the race visits along the way. The teams are progressively eliminated throughout the race at the end of most legs for being the last team to arrive at a designated Pitstop, 'The Mat'.

We hit the ground running after finding out that we've been successful. Filming will commence in just one month so we waste no time getting 'Race Ready'. For the next four weeks we live and breathe everything *Amazing Race*. We binge as many episodes as we can from all the different seasons around the world. We up our fitness and begin training twice a day, incorporating as much cardio as possible into our workouts. We spend hours and hours researching all the countries in the world, their capital cities and their flags. We know from watching the show that contestants are always tested on puzzles and memory challenges, so whenever we're not at the gym, we strengthen our skills with a variety of different games. I learn how to drive a manual car, how to change a tyre and even how to reverse a trailer. Basically, I release my inner straight man. It feels like we're a part of a month-long *Amazing Race* bootcamp, prepping for every possible scenario they could throw at us.

After training and planning for the entire month, the time comes to say goodbye to our parents, the only people we were allowed to tell, and make our way to Sydney to begin filming. To our surprise, on our arrival we are immediately locked in a hotel room. Our devices are confiscated and we're not allowed to leave the room unless people from production come and get us for meals, an hour of daily exercise in the gym or race-related admin. *Hardcore!* When we do leave the room, Rod and I aren't allowed to talk to anyone and the second we finish eating our meals in the restaurant or working out in the gym we're taken back up to our hotel room and locked in. We both feel like Rapunzel, locked away in her tower, and I'm sure if we didn't have each other to do what newlyweds do, we'd completely lose our minds. The amusing part is we never know when we're going to be called for a photoshoot or just a race update so the number of times the production crew almost catch us in the act is hilarious.

After what feels like forever being locked away in our rooms – actually only a few days – we're notified that we have the morning to pack our bags before we all head to the airport to fly to the official *Amazing Race* start line. We're surprised because we assumed we would start in Sydney. Then the bus takes a turn for the international terminals at Sydney airport and we're all like, whoa, where are we going?

As we enter the international terminal a producer gathers all the teams together and says, 'We're all about to board a plane to the start line of *The Amazing Race*, which will be in Seoul, South Korea.' We all erupt in a mixture of screams and gasps. *This is going to be one wild adventure.*

The race is one of the most incredible experiences of our lives. The sensation of adrenaline pumping through your veins every second of every single day is indescribable. Every time we rip open one of the clues, it is the biggest thrill ever and feels like a thousand Christmases have all come at once. We're completely thrown into the unknown and quickly have to learn to roll with the punches and fully immerse ourselves in every challenge. The best way to describe the race is like an insane never-ending roller coaster of emotions. You have the best days of your life and you have the worst days of your life. We feel so grateful to have been given the chance to participate.

The start line in Seoul, South Korea, is like stepping into one of our wildest dreams. The start line is always our favourite part. We're standing alongside ten other teams all waiting to start a race around the world. We have no idea where we're going in the world but the thing we all have in common is knowing it will be one hell of a crazy adventure. As we gaze around our surrounds, we are impressed to see the diverse teams of people we'll be racing against. Standing alongside us are people from every walk of life. We have AFL Players, Greek siblings, alpaca farmers. There are social media 'influencers', an Aboriginal duo from Gunditjmara and Larrakia peoples in the Northern Territory, and even two nuns, yes NUNS! This show is representing every type of Australian imaginable and we are so proud.

Everyone is there to win, and the atmosphere is electric. As we all stand nervously waiting for the countdown to begin, we're surrounded by what feels like hundreds of cameras. Every team has their own allocated sound and camera people along with the sea of other cameras capturing everything we do. Behind the cameras are multiple producers, cast managers and of course the executive director. It just doesn't feel real. Here we are in the hustle and bustle of Seoul, with local people walking past us all on their way to work. As the show's host, Beau Ryan, steps forward, he reminds us all to 'Race hard and race smart' then begins the countdown.

'Three, two, one, GO!' he screams and we are off. We will be the first legally gay married couple on Australian reality television, and we don't want to let anyone down. We sprint to our backpacks, which have been placed in a huge pile about 100 metres away. As the teams wrestle each other to reclaim their bags, we grab our first clue and rip it open. The race is officially on.

We visit locations we never in our wildest dreams thought

we would see: the rugged plains of Africa, the vast desert dunes of Mongolia, the majestic mountain ranges of Vietnam and the hustling metropolis of Bangkok. We even go to the border between North and South Korea. It's crazy, like something out of a movie, and we couldn't be happier – not that we have time to enjoy them because we are stressed out of our minds most of the time!

Although the race is incredibly tough, we have a fire in our bellies that keeps us going. We're determined to win for all the outcasts of society. We are racing for all the people who have ever felt different and like they don't fit in. We are racing for all the underdogs who feel like they are not good enough. From the very beginning we have channelled our inner warriors and we want to not just make our community proud but also motivate anyone who has ever felt different to never give up. We are racing for something much bigger than ourselves, and this helps to push us through all the roadblocks, detours and U-turns that are thrown our way.

We use the law of attraction all the time while we're competing on the race. Every single day we write notes to each other stating that we are the winners and that we will eventually take out the title. We speak our success out to the universe, and we honestly believe that along with our hard work and perseverance this will help us across the line in the end. We are using the power of our minds to translate our positive thoughts into a materialised reality.

The race just keeps getting better and better as it goes along, and teaches us new things every day. We both thrive on adventure and on this race there is a never-ending amount of it around every single corner. We learn things about each other that we never knew before. We improve our communication skills and try our hardest to stay cool under pressure, which I struggle with a lot more than Rod does. Every day is filled with challenges that we never thought possible. Some days are harder than others. On a few of the legs we race from the early hours of the morning into the night. Other days we race through the night and are so sleep deprived and jetlagged that we can't think straight. It feels like we're being thrown into a random country and then swept back up and spat out into another one on the other side of the globe. On the very few 'rest' days we have in which to recover, we are locked up in a hotel room and shut off from the world completely.

Racing almost becomes like a drug to us. The second we get to the mat, are checked in and told we're not going home, we come crashing straight back down to earth. After running on nothing but adrenaline for the past twenty-four hours, suddenly every single muscle aches. However, the next morning, no matter how run-down, tired and sore we are, the second we rip open the clue an indescribable wave of pure energy fills every ounce of our bodies. We never want this to end. But as we get further and further into the race it sinks in that no matter how far we make it, soon enough the race will officially be over.

It is the final day of the race and we're in the Northern Territory. There are only three teams left and we feel so lucky and privileged to be one of them, but we need to stay laser-focused and not make a single mistake. After a full day of Roadblocks and Detours, it's time for the very last challenge of the race.

We are dropped off by helicopter smack bang in the heart of Nitmiluk Gorge, which is a tunnel of enormous ancient sandstone cliffs. Our final challenge is to complete a near-impossible wooden puzzle in the scorching hot Australian sun. The puzzle is something out of our worst nightmares. Based on the clues written and pictured on the puzzle pieces, we need to separate them all by the countries they represent. Once we have figured that out, we need to assemble the six country-themed cubes. Finally, we have to carefully stack them up to receive our final clue.

Yes, each individual wooden piece of the puzzle has a small image on it. The image is either a country flag, another eliminated team or a particular challenge. The task is to not only build the six wooden cubes but build them with the correct wooden pieces from each individual country. This is a puzzle sent straight from hell, and we feel like we're up shit creek without a paddle.

Hours later and the final three teams are neck and neck. It's anyone's game; all it will take is for one of the teams to have a breakthrough with their puzzle pieces and they could win the challenge. After hours in the sweltering sun, we finally complete one of the six cubes of the puzzle. Now all we need to do is repeat exactly what we did with the first cube another five times, and we will have finished the entire puzzle. With our hands shaking and sweat dripping from every part of our bodies, we construct cube after cube. We briefly snap out of the intense puzzle trance we have been in for the past few hours and look around. The other teams are gaining ground and we need to keep our heads in the game and not miss a beat.

All we need to do now is build the final cube of the puzzle and then carefully stack all the cubes on top of each other, then we will receive our last clue and be in the lead. With trembling fingers we slot together the last pieces. Now it's time to stack our enormous cube tower. We slowly start placing the cubes on top of one another. The cube tower must stay standing on its own when fully completed without anything holding it up, or we won't receive the final clue.

We place the sixth and final cube on the wooden tower and slowly step away. If the puzzle tower falls we'll have to start all over again and possibly blow our chance of winning. We are both holding our breath, staring at the tower – I swear we are trying to hold it up with our eyes! To our joy it remains intact and we are handed the last clue, which reads, 'This is your last clue for *The Amazing Race Australia*. Search the gorge on foot to find Beau [the host] at the Finish Line! The first team to arrive will win $250,000.'

The other teams are completing their puzzles now. We are completely exhausted, jetlagged and run-down from weeks of racing nonstop around the world. However, the second we read this final clue our fuel tanks are instantaneously filled straight back up. I'm immediately overcome with the most insane energy boost I've ever experienced in my life. This will be our very last hurdle before we could potentially win. All we needed to do is race on foot through the gorge to find the final Pitstop, but we have no idea where to run. *OMG we are lost!*

We are in an enormous gorge, rocks everywhere. We can't see Beau, we can't see a mat, we don't know where we're running. The other teams are catching up! 'Run mate, run mate! We can do this!' I scream with every last bit of determination and encouragement I had within me.

We have put everything we have into this race. As we round a section of the gorge, we hear a loud cheer from the eliminated teams and then we see it – the final Pitstop with the other teams gathered around cheering us in. All we need to do now is hit the mat and we have won.

We grab each other's hands with tears welling in our eyes. It feels like I have endured a lifetime of not feeling good enough and like I was a total social outcast but here I am, about to win a race around the world hand in hand with the man of my dreams.

The eliminated teams are cheering madly and the sound is echoing throughout the gorge. We run as fast as we can, grasping each other's hand so tightly. As we run towards the Pitstop we can see multiple cameras all pointed at the final mat. A drone flying overhead captures every moment and the entire show's crew is clapping in excitement for us. This is the final moment of the relentless race around the globe, and we are seconds away from finding out if we will be crowned the champions.

We take one last step forward and jump onto the mat together, totally in sync, like we have done at every previous leg of the race. Then BOOM, complete and utter silence. As the echoes of the clapping and cheering from the other teams and crew subside Rod and I are left standing face to face with Beau. My mouth has dropped open in shock and I cover it with my hand as we anxiously wait for him to speak.

Beau declares, 'Tim and Rod, you are the winners of *The Amazing Race Australia*!' We both let out a scream. *OMG, we have done it, we have won the race!* I think we're both in shock.

Winning the race is one of the proudest moments of my life. I've spent so long feeling like I'm not good enough. But in this winning moment, I feel a sense of self-validation, that I am good enough as I am. Winning the race proves to that terrified little gay boy I once was that I deserve happiness and success in my life, and that I have finally found the willpower to achieve it.

The incredible sense of pride we both feel is not only from winning the race but also for representing the first married gay couple on prime-time TV. Of course our end goal was always to win the race and take home the money and the title, but we also wanted to help inspire and encourage people to be themselves, too. During the race we were dubbed 'the newlyweds' and it makes us so happy to think that our love being showcased on television might hopefully help normalise same-sex marriage within society. The fact that every week, families around Australia have been tuning into the show and seeing two husbands, two best mates, supporting, encouraging and loving each other is one of the most fulfilling aspects of the whole experience for us.

Another one of our main goals for appearing on the show was to help broaden the representation of gay people in the entertainment industry, to break free from the stereotype most frequently seen on television. Growing up, we both knew we were gay but really struggled to relate to anyone on television or in the media. Every clichéd gay man we saw on TV made us even more confused as we did not fit this stereotype. By taking part in *The Amazing Race*, we challenged expectations and hopefully made people question the cookie-cutter gay man persona they commonly see on TV. Rod and I want to show Australia and the world two proud gay best mates in love, and that at the end of the day if you have the courage to be yourself you can achieve anything. We want other LGBTQIA+ people or anyone who feels like an outcast or who may be struggling with their own journey to watch the show and have a sense of hope for the future.

We know what it's like to be lost and alone with no one to look up to and we want to be that glimmer of hope for other people. We hope that struggling LGBTQIA+ people can feel inspired to be themselves and one day potentially have the strength to be their authentic self with their family and friends.

Winning *The Amazing Race* is a huge metaphor for our lives.

It represents the struggles we've both been through and the physical and mental battles we've both overcome. It reinforces what we have learned the hard way: no matter how difficult, challenging and simply shit life can get, never give up and never ever lose track of your dreams, however outrageous they may be.

Epilogue

Life after *The Amazing Race* is surreal. We're constantly stopped in the street and recognised everywhere we go. People yell out, 'Tim and Rod!' Kids run up to tell us that we were their favourite team and take photos with us – yes, the Newlyweds, the Gay Team, was their favourite team. How is this possible? The two Newcastle boys who were either bullied for their sexuality or hated themselves because of it have won a race around the world and Australia is celebrating them for being themselves!

We feel so proud. We went into the race with the hope of making a difference to the lives of younger LGBTQIA+ people or anyone who feels they're different. We wanted to change at least one person's perception of what it is to be in a same-sex couple and normalise it, so that one day there isn't this immense pressure for young people to 'come out' – instead they can just be accepted and celebrated for who they are. We think we've made some progress and have encouraged open conversations in families and households.

We receive an enormous amount of love and support through social media. The comments that make our hearts so happy are the ones from teenage queer people who have told us that we inspire them and give them the courage to be themselves. They tell us that they'd never seen anyone they could relate to on TV until they saw us. Mums reach out to thank us for being role models for their young queer kids, and tell us we've given them hope and reassurance that their child will be okay.

Being in the public eye also has its struggles. People judge everything you do and say; we unfortunately get a ton of hate from homophobic and religious people telling us to 'burn in hell'. But we've grown a thick skin and by standing up to the haters we hope to set an example to young people who may be struggling, to send the message that they can celebrate their differences and embrace who they are. There is no way on Earth we're going to let haters bully us back into the closet.

No matter where you're at, whether you're finding yourself attracted to boys or girls or someone who's non-binary or gender diverse – or you simply just don't know yet – that's okay. You may feel like you're just different and that's okay, too.

If you're a parent, guardian or grandparent struggling with how to help a child working through their sexuality, we encourage you to simply love them unconditionally without judgement, listen to them and things will work out.

We always felt so alone and that we had no one to talk to or confide in, but we were wrong. We wish we could have taken our own advice and reached out to the appropriate people for help. It's okay to ask for help, and you deserve that help.

If you're in a dark place, you're not alone. For Australian readers, please reach out to Lifeline anytime on 13 11 14 or make an appointment to talk to your local health professional.

For more direct assistance for our beautiful LGBTQIA+ community, please call Qlife on 1800 184 527 or reach out to any of the following Australian organisations for a safe space to talk.

It's our hope that this book helps people in the same situation that we were in. Society has come a long way in accepting diverse people, but some of us still feel forced to put up a front – sometimes to protect ourselves from sideways glances, judgement, hurt, and sometimes just because it's what is expected of us.

No matter who you are, you're never going to be able to please everyone. And that's okay. Embrace who you are and know that your people are out there. They could be anywhere – another state, a different social group – but they're out there. Sometimes, they're just one suburb away.

When you find someone you love for who they are and they love you for you, it's an amazing feeling. But when you learn to love yourself for who you are, it's the greatest feeling in the world.

Headspace

https://headspace.org.au
Headspace is the National Youth Mental Health Foundation providing early intervention mental health services to twelve to

twenty-five year olds. It can help young people with their mental and physical health, and is committed to embracing diversity and eliminating all forms of discrimination in the provision of health services. Headspace welcomes all people irrespective of ethnicity, lifestyle choice, faith, sexual orientation and gender identity.

Minus18

https://minus18.org.au

Minus18 are champions for LGBTQIA+ youth in Australia, leading change, building social inclusion and advocating for an Australia where all young people are safe, empowered and surrounded by people who support them.

Black Rainbow

https://blackrainbow.org.au

Black Rainbow is Australia's leading Indigenous suicide prevention and mental health support service for LGBTQIA+ people. It is a 100 per cent Indigenous owned non-profit that provides support through a variety of community initiatives that it calls Contagion of Love projects.